Learn to Coach

Learn to Lead

Grow Your Sales, Team, Business, and Yourself
by Transforming from Manager to Coach

Sean Kelley

En Route Books and Media, LLC
Saint Louis, MO USA

Make the time

En Route Books and Media, LLC
5705 Rhodes Avenue
St. Louis, MO 63109

Contact us at **contact@enroutebooksandmedia.com**

Cover Credit: Chas Kelly

Copyright 2023 Sean Kelley

ISBN-13: 979-8-88870-098-3
Library of Congress Control Number: 2023946494

All rights reserved. No part of this book may be adapted, reproduced, stored in a retrieval system, or transmitted in any form, or by any means, electronic, mechanical, photocopying, or otherwise, without the prior written permission of the author.

Dedication

To all you aspiring managers, executives and business owners out there who understand that everyone you manage, is also someone you have a chance to lead.

Acknowledgments

To all my amazing and loyal coaching clients. You are so much more to me than "clients". We've been through pandemics and recessions. We've laughed, cried, and lost some, but mostly won! After all we've been through, we always get stronger, sell more and grow! The bottom line is, if it weren't for your openness to personal growth, I wouldn't be able to live out my life's purpose through you and your people every day. It's an honor to be your friend and coach. I wouldn't want to spend one minute of my life doing anything else with anyone else, but you! In the appendix of this book, you can likely find your name and last initial.

Thank you to my Coach Keith Rosen for setting me on this path. Thank you to my wife, Monica, because our success wouldn't be possible without you. Thank you to the Car Motivators and Market Motivators teams—you ensure we accomplish our mission each day. With your help, we will make our unified vision to positively impact the leadership landscape of managers across America a reality.

Table of Contents

Introduction 1

Chapter 1: Get Your Mind Right for Coaching 17
    Camp Pennsylvania, Kuwait, March 2003 18
    Think about this. What really got Hatem out of that jail cell? 23

Chapter 2: Understand what Coaching is NOT 27
    The Raven Paradox 27
    A Telling Problem 31
    The Selling Problem 32
    The Yelling Problem 34
    Are you giving Therapy or Coaching? 36
    Coaching is NOT a Reprimand or Punishment 38

Chapter 3: Understand what Coaching IS 43

Chapter 4: Set Your GPS 53
    Purpose 54
    Commission Structures Can and Will Change 58
    Find Out What They Want 82
    Uncover Their Strengths 86
    Create Opportunity 86
    Set Realistic Expectations 87

Measure Progress 87
Meet Other Needs 88

Chapter 5: The First Type of Coaching: Aspirational Coaching 103
    D - Discover What They Want in the Future and What They Want Now 105
    R - Recruit Them to Your Conversation 108
    I - Inquire to Build the Puzzle 112
    V - Verify You've Found their Missing Puzzle Piece and that it's Time to Add Value 122
    E - Educate – Bring Forth from Within (Ect Duco) 124
    C – Co-Create the Action Plan and Commit to it 130
    C - Confirm the Value of Coaching: Did they Get what they Wanted? 138
    C - Care for the Plan Long Term 142
    D.R.I.V.E.C3™ Coaching Convo Start to Finish 151

Chapter 6: The Second Type of Coaching: Metric Coaching 163

Chapter 7: The Third Type of Coaching: Observational Coaching ... 171
    The Tools of Observational Coaching 173
    Rules of Engagement for Observational Coaching 176
    Steps for Effective Observational Coaching Conversations 177
    Triple Loop Learning 182
    Observational Coaching Can Happen at Any Time 185

Table of Contents

Chapter 8: The Fourth Type of Coaching: Turn Around Coaching .. 189
Recruit them to the Conversation 190
Commit to Turn Around Coaching 191
Detach from the Outcome 196

Chapter 9: Coaching around Limiting Beliefs 199
What is a Limiting Belief? 199
Why Do Limiting Beliefs Exist? 201
The Four Mistakes You Must Avoid When Dealing With Limiting Beliefs 201
Tactics for Coaching Around Limiting Beliefs 203
What's Holding Us Back? 226

Chapter 10: Measuring Success through Coaching 235
Creating a Coaching Culture 236
Track Coaching Consistency 239
Create Coaching Wins and Duplicate Success 242

Chapter 11: Inspired Satisfaction 247
Inspired Satisfaction: How to Get More Motivation from Everyone and Predict Employee Turnover 247
Impact on the Rest of the Team 248
Impact on Customer Retention 249
Predict the Future 249

Chapter 12: Creating Your Coaching Cadence 255

    Coaching Buys Back Your Time 256

    Empower Your Employees to Think for Themselves 265

    Understand the Coaching Capacity Necessary for Your Team ... 270

    Build a Coaching Cadence Calendar 271

Chapter 13: Onward and Upward 273

Appendix: Leadership Acknowledgments 283

Introduction

My name is Sean Kelley, and I am a Special Operations combat veteran. I am also a husband of 15 years to a phenomenal woman named Monica. I am a father of three amazing kids, Jack, Ava, and Emma Kelley. I am a man of faith and a business leader who is blessed enough to live out my purpose every single day. My purpose is to bring massive value to the lives of others by helping them achieve what they want most in their career and their lives as their personal career coach.

I humbly admit that I am one of the top sales and leadership coaches in the country, and in the last twelve months of writing this I have been ranked number 10 in the "100 Sales Coaches to Watch" by Ambition.com, consultant of the year by dealershipnews.com, and have spoken hundreds of times across North America at technology companies, car dealerships, associations, and conferences on sales, business operations, business culture and, my true passion, leadership coaching and people development.

I am on a mission to bring coaching to the car business, and my vision is to have positively impacted the leadership landscape of the entire automotive industry. While who I am now is important to this book, who I was before I became a coach is equally important. I didn't start off with influence, connections, money, management skills, leadership skills, or any other sort of head start. I was just a normal kid with A.D.D. from a small town in the Midwest. Yet the road I did travel down which transformed me from manager to coach had a profound impact on my sales team, my business, my life, and now the lives and careers of thousands of people I am blessed enough to coach every day from coast to coast.

What that means for you is that it doesn't matter your level of experience in leadership, your current status, or your coaching skills (or lack thereof). All that matters is that if you choose to take the same path I did, you will transform as a leader, make a greater difference in the lives of your personnel than you can imagine, and it is likely that your life may be positively changed forever.

As a senior level manager at the top Hyundai store in St. Louis, I was able to receive the coaching necessary to become the leader my team needed. I was able to develop the coaching skills, language, and processes which helped my team and me succeed at a level beyond what I thought was possible. All of which I share in detail within this book. These skills helped our store which was number one in St. Louis rise to first time regional first place finishes. That's like going from little league to major league almost overnight. In our local market, our manufacturer was down by well over 14%. The people development best practices contained within this book helped us become the only volume store up in that down market for two years straight. In fact, even in this down market we were setting 1st place regional records against hundreds of competitors.

If you're worried about a market downturn, if you are experiencing one now, or if you just believe business growth is possible, the principles in this book will help you thrive, regardless. Perhaps the greatest victory was eliminating unhealthy turnover from my business. A recent N.A.D.A. (North American Dealer Association) study calculated one lost salesperson costs a dealership $7,500 dollars. Based on the time, energy, and pain I experienced when recruiting, rehiring, and retraining employees, I believe it's thousands more than that. Whatever your industry, when you learn and implement the techniques contained within this book, you will be able to hire and retain employees.

What I want for you in reading this book is to help you enjoy the same success and achievements. I want for you and your team to be equally impacted by what you will read and implement in this book. My plan is to help you start your journey down the same road to success and more. In fact, my goal is to help you reach your desired destination in the shortest amount of time by giving you the most comprehensive roadmap ever written on coaching.

This book will first help you truly define what coaching is and is not. Only by truly understanding what coaching is and is not can you leverage its amazing power to grow your business and truly maximize your career and the success of each person on your team. Next you will learn about four specific types of coaching, the benefits to implementing each, and each of the four coaching processes. These processes will help you get practical and tactical and ensure your coaching conversations have real measurable impact. Real life documented coaching conversations that fit each of the four types of coaching will be shared in this book. In that way, you can better understand the coach's mindset and the relationship between the coach and coachee. You will also see the tangible measured results that came from each coaching conversation so that you can understand the ridiculously high possible returns on your investment in learning and leveraging effective coaching. Most importantly, you will understand the impact that each of these conversations had on the well-being of the person being coached.

Next, you will begin to master the language of coaching when learning what works as it relates to holding effective coaching conversations. Also, to ensure you don't spin your wheels for months like I did when I made my first attempt at coaching my employees, the obstacles to coaching success will be identified, as well as how to avoid and overcome each of them. You will be able to effectively coach and improve even the most stubborn and challenging employees.

If you are reading this book, you are probably a lot like I used to be, successful in spite of myself. Throughout my first 15 years in the car business, I was a salesperson, a finance manager, a used car manager, a general sales manager, and while my career growth trajectory looked great, I was also extremely frustrated. The frustration came from many reasons. I wanted to move up in my company and be offered an ownership position. We had nine dealerships in our organization, and I wanted to be the number one manager in the group. For that to happen, I needed my store to set sales records. Most important to me was that I wanted everyone on my sales team to succeed and thrive under my leadership. I wanted all of my people to be able to give their families the lives that they deserved, and that required selling more, in less time, so they could find better "work-life balance". I felt like I could never get everything done I needed to get accomplished. I wanted to eliminate turnover at my dealership. It pained me to lose employees that couldn't hack it selling. I wanted to make sure everyone on my team achieved their greatest potential. And I spent ten years managing with these frustrations, beating my head against the wall trying to figure out how to achieve those things.

The reason accomplishing this level of success was so important to me was because of the way I grew up. As a child, I had a father who loved us very much but suffered from severe sleep apnea. This led to his being tired all the time which cascaded into depression. As such, my father couldn't hold down a job. This led to my family of six siblings living extremely impoverished. It wasn't uncommon for our water or electric to be shut off due to nonpayment. There was a time when my stepmother was making eight dollars an hour at an art store, and with those low wages and my father's lack of any, we couldn't afford full meals. I remember a time where we had the need to eat Cheez-Its for dinner when the pantry was almost empty. As a result of the financial stress, much arguing ensued. Marriages under that level of stress don't often last, and this led to divorce. I grew up hearing over and over, "If only your Dad could keep a job…" and "If only he helped contribute to the finances…"

Due to this past, I had a burning desire to achieve massive success in my career, and I was willing to do more honest hard work than most to make that happen. Working sixteen-hour days wasn't uncommon for me, which wasn't conducive to being a great husband or father. Yet all the desire and work ethic in the world wasn't enough to get what I wanted. Nor was it enough to create a healthy, happy, centered leader; I needed a roadmap to achieve it. I became frustrated. The frustration set in because it seemed that the only way to get better results was to work harder. I felt like I couldn't work harder because I was already putting in sixteen hours or more per day. In fact, one night I was up late pricing cars in my inventory while lying in bed. I didn't notice the time until my wife rolled over in bed and asked me, "Is your life insurance up to date?"

I asked, "Why?" as I looked over at the clock. It was two in the morning.

She said, "Because people that work as much as you don't live very long."

To her it was just a passing comment, but that statement affected me. I reflected on her statement for days, if not weeks. I couldn't figure out why her statement bothered me for some time. I didn't mind hard work, nor was I afraid of death. One day I realized it bothered me because I realized that I was ineffective and inefficient as a manager and a leader. It seemed like no matter how much I wanted to get everything done that needed to get done at the office, it just wasn't possible. Inside, I felt like I could never unplug, relax, and really enjoy time at home with my family. Anytime I would try to detach from work, it was on my mind. In the few circumstances when I was off work and not thinking about it, I would have to field calls from customers and employees who needed my help. After ten years in a management role, I wouldn't have ever thought it possible coaching could take my team to the next level. A level of success where I could get everything done, my team didn't rely on me as a crutch, and I could enjoy setting records at work while relishing in focused time with my family.

While my mission is to bring coaching to the car business, I want you to know that the principles within this book will help you coach your team to success in any leadership role for any industry. The first reason I am so confident in this is because I have coached and trained hundreds of managers to learn the language of coaching in technology, marketing, non-profit, automotive, and service industries. The second reason for my confidence is due to the retail car business being one of the fastest-paced, most random, reactive, and chaotic businesses in America, if not the world. If coaching can bring order, growth, consistency, focus, and less stress to that world, then it can multiply that same impact elsewhere. When you are a sales manager at a dealership, it is chaos from the moment you hit the showroom floor to the moment you go home at night (or the next morning when sometimes working past midnight).

It's not uncommon to have to deal with messed up paperwork from the finance department preventing a loan from being funded, an angry customer wanting to return their car, a salesperson asking for help because they didn't know what to do about a customer who didn't get floor mats in their car, two salespeople needing a proposal with multiple lease and finance options printed, three cars to appraise before we could work a deal, the service manager lined up to go over the seven used car service bills, a bank rep stopping by to ask when we will send them some loans, the owner calling to find out why we didn't log the deals from the weekend (of course, the internet had gone out so this wasn't possible and still wasn't up yet), our marketing director asking for the updated new car price list, and our lot manager wanting to know what to do about the car that just had the antennae broken off in the car wash. Did I mention it's not even 10:30 a.m., yet? If you had told me then that I would find a way to control this chaos and spend 40 hours per month conducting career and life changing one-on-ones with every one of my direct reports, I would have laughed and called you crazy. Now, when I work with executives and senior leaders, I enjoy the same reaction from them when sharing that we will make this their reality through coaching.

By the time I had become a GSM in the auto industry, I had spent almost two years in combat zone deployments in the Army. Seven months in Bosnia, Operation Joint Forge, then a fourteen-month deployment to Iraq, Operation Iraqi Freedom 1 as an NCO (Non-Commissioned Officer) in a leadership position. I was able to keep everyone alive in combat, yet as a manager I was finding it much harder to keep salespeople gainfully employed at my dealership long-term. I was like most sales managers battling an industry average of 71% turnover, and I wanted to find a way to eliminate this from my dealership. In fact, the bottom 20% of my sales team constantly turned over, leading our store to a 90% employee turn over. It was exceedingly frustrating and time consuming to find the replacements and then deal with ramping them up. I had the belief that it was hard to find good employees, and as such I would hire them and (to coin auto industry lingo), "Throw 'em against the wall to see if they stick."

You see, I wanted to retain the salespeople and service advisors on my team because I knew that losing employees was costing me sales, money, and frustration trying to replace them. Every time I lost an employee it really bothered me, and I wondered, "Why can I keep soldiers alive in combat, but I can't keep salespeople at my dealership?" I would recruit and hire out of desperate need for

Introduction

people and as such hire almost anyone who interviewed. This created a situation where we would often bring the wrong people into the company which slowed down our success. I needed a strategy that would all but eliminate this turnover and ensure the right people were brought into the business and retained in the right way. I would have been all over it. I later realized that my problem wasn't my inability to find good people, but my inability to develop them that was holding me back. Lucky for me, I found that strategy in coaching.

While I was a believer in training, I had a hard time getting the 80% of my sales team who were sales veterans to buy-in to taking training. After all, these people had already heard what I had to say and how I personally sold cars dozens of times in sales meetings over the years. These people had mostly plateaued in results and were meeting volume and profit expectations, and training didn't seem to make them better. Not to mention, they were usually busy with customers when it was training time and I would let them skip it. When they did come to training, they did it begrudgingly and would say they would have one or two takeaways, but it never moved the needle on their results.

If someone had told me then that there was a way to get buy-in from my top producing salespeople and seasoned veterans and give them personal development that impacted their results, I would have been pretty skeptical. Later, through coaching, I was able to help my seasoned veterans develop their results and grow to new heights of sales success. Now, I help salespeople of any tenure across the country grow theirs and teach their sales managers to do the same.

Even though I had reached the level of GSM, I still wanted to move up in the company to Owner Operator, General Manager or even become a multi-store sales director. I felt stuck because our nine-store group didn't have General Manager positions. The owners were brothers in their 50s and were very active and involved with the company. I made the assumption that the owners didn't want to have GMs because they didn't want to pay the salary. In addition to that, there were many other managers who had been with the company longer. The owners had family members in leadership roles within the organization, which led me to believe surely my chances of being promoted ahead of them were slim to none. Little did I know that the coaching journey I would take would create so many more possibilities. The coaching journey would take me even further than being offered a General Manager position, to being offered a position of owner and partner by my current dealership and others that I've been blessed enough to coach for.

My desire to bring home the gold medal by being the most successful store was strong. I wanted to sell the most cars, be the most profitable dealership, and be known as the best manager in my group. I really wanted that first place ribbon for my store's employees, too. When it came to setting records, as you can probably tell from most of the stories and mindsets I've already shared, this was going to be tough to do. This was especially since my dealership group had nine stores, and each one had competitive and talented sales managers running them. Some of them had been with the company for thirty years and were part of much more popular franchises that captured more market share. Some of our stores were in better locations. Some stores had brand new buildings that made the Taj Mahal look like a shanty.

The odds were stacked against me, but even though I didn't know how, I knew it was possible to be the #1 leader and maximize my team's potential. My belief is that there is always a solution to every problem, always a way to accomplish the mission. I remember the quote the famous French writer Voltaire had said, "No problem can withstand the onslaught of sustained thinking."

I was up for figuring out the challenge because I had always been known for taking the difficult road. It was not knowing how to achieve the win that was my barrier. Once I learned what I needed to learn, the process of and leadership language of coaching, and applied the principles to my leadership routine, we were able to remain the only volume store up in a down market, set first time records like #1 certified pre-owned and #1 new car sales in the region, all while cutting our advertising in half. Creating a coaching culture helped us become the most profitable store in our dealer group.

Everything within this book took me years of failure and success to learn, develop, test, enhance, and improve. The processes within are not just some random things I decided to make up one day. First, I spent years failing as a manager. I spent years failing as a husband and father putting work above all else. All before spending months reading dozens of books on coaching. Then I spent months upon months failing as I tried to coach, and each of those failures taught me something valuable and made me a better coach as I reflected on my coaching efforts and received coaching from some of the best coaches in the world.

After my coaching began to make a massive impact, it still wasn't enough for me to write this book. I needed hundreds if not thousands of coaching wins in order to have the confidence to share it all with you. Everything within this book is based on real coaching conversations from real world leadership and sales challenges that were coached on, followed up with, supported, and produced measurable results, over and over for different managers and sales teams in different markets and businesses from coast to coast and even in Canada. As much as I have had a desire to write this book sooner, I needed to ensure everything I shared was concrete, proven, and factual before moving forward.

What you must also understand before diving into this book is what I call the compound knowledge effect. I describe compound knowledge as the premise that when you combine multiple pieces of lower impact knowledge the effects compound into something spectacular. The compound knowledge that caused me to focus like a laser on coaching my team came from a variety of books and lessons learned. One day the owner of my company sat in on one of my run-of-the-mill sales meetings. After the meeting, he came to me and said, "Sean, you should learn about coaching." I've always been good at following orders, so I did what he asked. Little did any of us know this one suggestion would change so many lives!

In addition to all my failures and successes combined with the constant question I kept asking myself, "What am I missing?" and the belief that there was a better way I just hadn't found yet, I read a book called *Coaching Salespeople Into Sales Champions* by Keith Rosen. Then I hired him to be my coach. Keith taught me the

"Why" and the "How" to coach, but it wasn't yet enough for me to make coaching my everything.

Next, I read a book called *Nine Minutes on Monday* by James Robbins. From it, I learned that there are nine employee-engagement needs and, if these are met, employees will run through brick walls for their managers. It alone wasn't enough for me to focus on coaching.

Then I read a book called *Killing the Sale: The 10 Fatal Mistakes Salespeople Make and How To Avoid Them* by Todd Duncan which helped me uncover my purpose, which is to help people get what they want most out of their careers.

Finally, I read a fourth book called *The One Thing* by Gary Keller and Jay Papasan. In it, I found out that there is always one thing you should be doing at any given moment in time that makes everything else easier or unnecessary. I pondered what my one thing was for some time, and then it hit me: coaching. Coaching would meet all employee engagement needs, which would inspire and motivate my employees. Coaching would make my people so good that they could do my job for me and free up my time to do more coaching for them. Coaching would fulfill my life's purpose of helping people get what they want most out of their career. Coaching was my one thing that would make everything else easier or unnecessary!

After doing just that for two consecutive years at my dealership, my life changed as did that of my employees. Sure, we set first time regional records, something that wasn't accomplished even when the owner of my company ran the store. In our market, Hyundai was down, and we were the only volume store up in that market for two consecutive years. More importantly, unhealthy turnover at my store was almost completely eliminated. The only people who were leaving were people being promoted or the ones who weren't a good fit for my company and/or team. Those were the people that coaching helped me realize that I shouldn't have hired in the first place.

The best results, and the ones I truly care most about, the results that set me on my mission to bring coaching to the car business were when one salesperson made me his child's Godfather. Another asked me to marry him and his fiancée on the showroom floor at our dealership, which I did with honor. I took these results as a sign, a sign that I had a greater responsibility than to that of my twenty-person team. People across the country needed to know how to do this as well, and I had to teach them. In the end, it was the compound knowledge of the key factors above and more that sent me on this journey.

I discovered the true impact of coaching, as you will learn throughout the coaching methodologies I share in this book. Through coaching the following are indeed possible for you, too: get it all done each day, enjoy more quality time with your family, reach new levels of success in your business, motivate and develop your top producers to achieve more, retain your employees, always hire the right employees, be the top manager in your dealership, set first time records, spend less money in advertising, earn promotions and grow your career all the way up to partner, become a software company executive, eliminate turnover, get everyone on your team to adopt a new technology tool or process, or anything else you choose to do in business or life for that matter.

Introduction

As you read through this book, you will notice several recurring themes that come up time and again. Because this book is designed to teach you how to coach, everything in it builds upon what came before, and I'm layering in more information as it goes along so you can see how it all connects.

Get excited and strap yourself in as you are about to not only positively impact your life but also the lives of everyone else around you as you learn the skills I am about to share with you! The leadership language of coaching! Your coaching journey begins here!

Chapter 1

Get Your Mind Right for Coaching

Everything I needed to succeed I learned from an Iraqi boy we found on the brink of starvation in a prison cell. Sound crazy? Well, it's true.

At the age of 17, I joined the military because growing up my grandfather would tell me war stories about his time in the Navy during World War II. He had lied about his age to join the military and found himself on board the Lexington. The Lexington was crippled by the Japanese attack in the Battle of Coral Sea during which fuel caught fire and began exploding throughout the ship.

My grandfather, while showing me some of his awards, explained how he did a swan dive off the deck and proceeded to rescue injured sailors from drowning. Wanting adventure and to be a hero like my grandfather, along with a strong sense of patriotism growing up in the Midwest, I decided to join the military at a young age. In fact, the first recruitment to get ahold of me closed the deal. I signed up for the Army at the age of 17 and a half.

The ASVAB test said I should be in Psychological Operations, and though I wasn't quite sure what this was, all I knew was that I enjoyed my high school psychology class, that there was a unit near my home in Missouri, and that there was a sizable bonus for that position. I knew in signing up for the military that there was a chance I could be deployed overseas but had no clue I was going to be part of one of the most deployed and high demand special operations careers in the military. As a result, I spent over two years in combat zone deployments including Bosnia and Iraq.

Camp Pennsylvania, Kuwait, March 2003

It was mid-March in 2003 and a few days before Operation Iraqi Freedom was to kick off. I was deployed to the Middle East.

From the moment we left Fort Bragg, North Carolina, where we had mobilized, everything changed. The government chartered us a civilian flight and flying overseas post 9/11 in full "battle rattle" carrying your fully automatic machine guns onboard a plane while being served drinks by a flight attendant was just surreal. Upon arrival in Kuwait, things became intense. After landing at dusk, our unit drove throughout the night trying to locate Camp Pennsylvania. There was immediate stress because the trip was supposed to be a couple hours, and it took much longer.

The war was scheduled to start any time within the next week, and we didn't know if we had hours or days to rendezvous with the unit we were supporting, the 101st Airborne. That night we drove what seemed aimlessly for hours trying to locate the camp where we would prep to cross the border with the 101st when the war kicked off.

After a sleepless night of driving, we found our way and arrived at Camp Pennsylvania moments before a 101st airborne soldier went berserk, stealing grenades from the armory and lobbing them into his commander's tent before shooting at fellow unprepared solders around the camp as they exited their tents to see what was going on. The camp was in chaos to say the least, and at the time we assumed it was an attack by Iraqi forces. We found out later what had really happened.

The next night the dust had almost settled. We were already exhausted from lack of sleep from the night before and prepping for combat we had done all day. I was excited to catch some sleep, but just as I was dozing off, a sound I had never heard up close and personal jarringly woke me and everyone else at the camp from our sleep. It sounded akin to a space shuttle launch at Cape Canaveral but was in fact a patriot missile battery launch. We were taught that Patriot missile batteries were set up to take out deadly SCUD missiles Iraqi forces would launch from Iraq. SCUD Missiles were known to not only cause large explosive damage, killing or maiming anyone within their blast radius, but also that they could carry chemical or biological weapons that Saddam had already used against enemy forces within his country in the past.

We immediately donned our chemical suits and gas masks and jumped into hastily made bunkers in an attempt to protect ourselves from SCUD missiles. After another sleepless night, we found out that the patriot missile battery had in fact reacted to a British aircraft and shot it down instead.

The next day we had heard that the war was going to kick off within 48 to 72 hours, and we were waiting for the call from General Petraeus. We thought we would have a couple days to get some rest and finish prepping. It was the third night at Camp Pennsylvania, and finally we were going to get some sleep... Or so we thought.

That night we were awakened by a salty Vietnam veteran special forces Sergeant. "PSY OP, let's go! We're crossing the border early!"

Before I could finish asking, "Where are we going Sergeant…" he cut me off.

"I'll tell you on our way. You have 30 minutes to get ready. LET'S GO."

We began our blacked-out drive, no headlights whatsoever, by cover of darkness and found out that there was an abandoned building that we were going to. Our mission was to travel to that building just south of the city Najaf where the first battle was to take place and remain there until before the fighting kicked off. We would use our mini cassette tape player with pre-recorded messages and our loudspeakers we carried with us or the speakers mounted to our vehicles to influence our target audience (the enemy) to surrender instead of fight, potentially saving countless lives. It was the latest technology at the time.

At this point sleep deprivation was causing me to hallucinate. I remember seeing Chevy Cavaliers pulling in and out of our convoy on the way there, which made no sense because Iraq didn't have those. Not to mention, we were driving through a dusty, treacherous desert that only offroad vehicles could traverse. Just before dawn we arrived at the "abandoned building". As we pushed the large metal door open, the worst smell I have ever experienced smacked me in the face.

Before I had time to wretch in disgust, our presence became known right away when we began hearing voices calling out in Arabic from inside. Screams of fear and terror and pleas for help echoed throughout the building. It wasn't an abandoned military building at all, but it turned out to be an occupied Iraqi prison. As it turned out, the Iraqi prison guards saw the U.S. mobilizing and decided to leave the jail for fear of being killed as the U.S. passed through on the road north to Baghdad. They left approximately 175 inmates locked up with no food or water for what we were told later was close to a week. Now the inmates didn't know if we were there to liberate them or execute them, and they were understandably freaked out about our presence.

Now that our position was compromised, we had to get out of there fast. As we were evacuating the building with the plan to return to our vehicles and make a hasty retreat, I heard a voice in English behind me. At first, I dismissed it as another hallucination. Then again, in perfect English I heard what sounded like a child's voice say, "Hey man, get me out of here!"

At the same time the Iraqis yelling had stopped, so maybe there was an American locked up inside? I brought it up to the team we were with and after ensuring our perimeter was secure and we weren't being attacked, we decided to go back into the Iraqi jail and see who was speaking English.

Inside we saw a horrible site that rivaled that of the WWII concentration camp photos. Everyone was famished; some had died. That being said, there were several Iraqis pointing at a skinny little boy who looked to be about 15 years old.

The salty Vietnam veteran sergeant looked at the kid and proclaimed, "Boy if you can understand what the fuck I am saying I'll get you the fuck out of here."

The young man looked up and respectfully replied, "I understand you say a lot of bad words, sir."

I chuckled at his unintentional humor.

"Get him out of there!" the Sergeant ordered.

I was a little concerned with this abrupt approach to freeing an unknown Iraqi inmate. So I asked, "Sergeant, what if he's the Hannibal Lecter of Iraq or something like that? He looks harmless, but should we do a little interrogation and see why he's in here?"

After some discussion, we found out that the boy's name was Hatem, and he had been locked up for almost 6 months at the age of 16. Saddam's sons Uday and Qusay had come through his village and killed three men. They took the wives and daughters of these men who were never seen again. After Hatem had called Saddam and his sons a bunch of monsters, Hatem's cousin told the local Ba'ath Party officials about his quip against them. In turn, Hatem had been locked in prison.

The special forces team knew we would need a strong Iraqi interpreter because our prerecorded cassette tape was neither efficient nor easy to use when the bullets were flying. Hatem joined us for our entire stint in Iraq. Throughout the next year, Hatem traveled with us everywhere we went and partook in every mission we ran. He did an amazing job as our interpreter, saving our lives on occasion, and helping us save the lives of many others as we would leverage his translation skills on both our loudspeakers, as well as in conversations with Iraqi officials as we worked to win the hearts and minds of the Iraqi population.

In fact, Hatem did such great work for us that General Petraeus himself decided to make Hatem his personal interpreter after we left Iraq. This led to Hatem interpreting between General Petraeus and Saddam Hussein just before Saddam was hung. This led to Hatem being brought to the U.S. to train soldiers and marines how to survive in Iraq and better interact with the local population. After that,

Chapter 1: Get Your Mind Right for Coaching

Hatem moved to St. Louis where I live and even worked for me as a very successful sales consultant at my dealership, and he is now a U.S. Citizen.

You may be asking, "What does this crazy story have to do with coaching and leadership?"

I believe every mindset you need to succeed in your business, and grow as a leader, you can learn from this young Iraqi boy.

Think about this. What really got Hatem out of that jail cell?

There are three things that helped free Hatem, three lessons that I took from him and applied to my life and business. These are the same three mindsets you will need to adopt if you want to learn to coach your team and truly gain the most from this book.

First, the willingness to stretch your comfort zone. Remember, neither Hatem nor the inmates within the prison knew why we were there. Hatem risked his life to call out in English to us. He could have remained frozen in terror or paralyzed by the fear of failure or being killed. When he chose to speak up, he chose to stretch his comfort zone.

This is critical for any leader who desires to master a new skill such as coaching. Because any time you begin a new skill, there will be some degree of discomfort. In fact, as you take on the new leadership behaviors I outline in detail in this book, it is likely you will need to adjust one or more of the following: your routine, the way you deliver your messages, how you follow up with each employee, how you measure success, how you give meetings, the depth of your relationships with your employees, your ability to listen, how you add value, how you learn, the way you set expectations with others, and more.

In short, take a lesson from Hatem, and get comfortable being uncomfortable. Since growth does not happen within your comfort zone, it's imperative that you consistently live outside its boundaries.

Second is your ability to communicate. Communication is the cornerstone and foundation for your success, your team's success, and your effectiveness as a leader. Nothing happens until communication takes place, and the right things can only happen with the right communication. Hatem was able to speak the same language as us and, as such, he was able to bring massive value. He stood out from the other inmates, and his ability to get his point across changed the course of his life, my life, and the lives of hundreds, if not thousands, of other people.

I used to think I was a good communicator. In fact, growing up and throughout my entire life everyone told me I should be in sales. The ASVAB test told me I should be in Psychological Operations, another indicator of good communication skills. I aced my speaking classes in high school and college. I used to give B.U.B. (Battle Update Briefings) to high-ranking officers while in the military. I was able to leverage the communication skills I had in the auto industry to become one of the top sellers within my dealer group and earn multiple promotions at both dealer groups I worked at. Yet, learning to coach taught me how poor my communication skills were.

Coaching taught me to identify the assumptions I was making while noticing these in others. Coaching helped me realize the attachments I had to outcomes and my inability to be objective and truly understand others' perspectives. Communicating effectively through coaching helped me understand the reality of situations which allowed me to focus my energy and efforts in the right areas of my life, my business, and my team.

How do you rank yourself as a communicator? Why do you give yourself that rating? Learn from Hatem and leverage this book to become the leader and communicator your team truly needs to achieve what you want most. It is the cornerstone of your success.

The third lesson I want you to learn from this story is to adopt what I call a "Growth Mindset". In Iraq it was more or less forbidden to learn English. Anti-American propaganda and constant fear of tyrannical dictatorship threatened people's lives and freedom. The last thing Saddam wanted were English speaking "spies". Hatem used to get beat up for trying to learn English. But neither fear, nor actual physical harm, could stop him from learning English! (Which he accomplished by watching Jim Carrey movies and reading subtitles.) But that didn't stop Hatem because he always wanted to, and always wants to grow as a person in values, character, and skills.

When I asked Hatem why he worked so hard to learn English when it wasn't even taught at his school, Hatem told me, "I never get tired of learning. Learning English just seemed like it made sense because the most successful countries in the world speak English, and if I can learn it, maybe I can grow my success one day."

Having a growth mindset is key for learning the leadership language of coaching because coaching is a gift that you give yourself and your team that drives growth. To be the most effective coach for each person on your team, you need to desire growth in the form of financial growth, skill mastery growth, results growth, career growth, growth for others' careers, growth for your supervisors or business you work at, growth for your family, growth in your relationships, etc. This means you are forever a student. You must be insatiably curious and ready to learn and implement new things.

I believe we are all like Hatem circa 2003, trapped in our own little Iraqi prison cells. Our ability to get free and achieve our version of success in our lives and businesses is directly related to our willingness to stretch our comfort zones, our ability to effectively communicate, and how strong our growth mindset is.

If you're still reading this, I'll take that as your signature on the dotted line to the commitment of learning to coach and that you have adopted ALL three mindsets from Hatem's story. Go ahead and post your #GrowthMindset photo holding this book on Facebook, LinkedIn, Instagram or other social media of your choice. Throw that hashtag in your post! If I find your picture online with that hashtag, you can expect me to reach out and say hello!

X_____ I am committed!

Chapter 2

Understand what Coaching is NOT

Coaching sometimes gets a bad rap. There are a few reasons for this. First, too many people confuse coaching with training. Training is teaching someone how to do something, and a great deal of that goes on with new hires both in the automotive industry and elsewhere. Training someone on procedures is not coaching. Second, people confuse coaching with correction or discipline. While coaching seeks to improve the quality of an employee, it is not the same as sitting down with your boss or HR and getting harangued about what you've done wrong now. Third, too many people who should be calling themselves trainers or managers are calling themselves coaches when they are not in fact coaches and are not providing that service. So, first, we need to get a handle on what coaching isn't before we can talk about what it is.

The Raven Paradox

Carl Hempel, the famous logician, created the Raven Paradox. His goal was to discredit what you can actually learn from a factual statement. Hempel's Paradox goes like this. "All ravens are black. All things that are not black are not a raven." Both of these sentences follow an equality logic, so if one is true, that means the other must also be true. If this is the case, then that means one is able to look at anything and everything, and as long as it isn't black, you can accurately claim that it's not a raven.

The paradox shows that in learning what something is not, you can also learn what something is. In this critical chapter, you will learn what coaching is not. In that way, you will honestly be able to know when you are coaching effectively and when you are not. You will also be able to find out from self-proclaimed coaches if they accurately know what coaching really is. As such, you will be able to protect coaching in its purest form by ensuring you can live up to and enact real coaching. After reading this chapter, you will be able to answer the following questions: What is coaching? What is not coaching? Why are some of my employees fearful of coaching, and how can I get around that fear? What if someone isn't coachable? Why is coaching so effective? What is the difference between training and coaching? Why is coaching critical to be paired with training?

In what I call the B.C. era (before coaching), I had the same routine for a decade for my weekly sales meetings as a sales manager. And boy, oh boy, did I use to give some sales meetings! If you could see my expression as I write this, I'm cringing while grabbing my forehead and shaking my head thinking about the way I used to conduct sales meetings. I digress, my routine was simple.

Throughout the week, I would write down some of the wins and losses, success stories and failures, and anything else that was important at the time and bring that to my sales meeting as an agenda. I would stand up in front of the team and go through each bullet point one by one. Basically, I would pontificate all over my team until I covered everything on my agenda. While I tried to make them educational, fun, and motivational, in retrospect it was a one-way dialogue with no conversation. I have no clue how my employees put up with it for so long without coming to the meeting with pitch forks and torches with the goal of tarring and feathering me.

In fact, we may owe this book's very existence to the crummy way I used to conduct my sales meetings. One day, the owner of my company, a savvy businessman by the name of Butch, came to one of my meetings. I was excited he was attending, and though I never found out the reason for his presence, afterward he pulled me aside and said, "Sean, you should learn about coaching."

I remember my exact, honest, yet jovial, response when I grinned at him and said, "Is coaching when you yell at everyone instead of one person?" While I was joking, I did realize at the time I couldn't accurately define coaching.

He chuckled and said, "Goodbye!"

In reality, I had no clue what coaching really was or wasn't. Sure, I had coaches in sports growing up. I remember running a lot of wind sprints with the rest of my team. I had also been "coached" when I screwed something up at work as a fourteen-year-old kid working at a restaurant. I was a bus boy, and during a busy brunch I mistook a car seat for a bus tub. I wiped the remnants of a family's breakfast into that car seat, which of course contained an infant. Only after nervously picking the pancake covered in syrup off of the baby's giggling face did I receive my first "coaching" conversation. The owner of the restaurant sat me down and wrote me up and said, "It's time for some coaching, Sean. Do something that stupid again and I'll fire you. Now sign here."

Did I deserve to be yelled at for my screw up? Absolutely! That being said, coaching did not deserve to be lumped into a bucket with that sort of management activity. In fact, if we use the Raven Paradox, and I were to say, all one-way conversations where the manager is telling, selling, or yelling are NOT coaching, then you can avoid calling something that's not coaching, coaching. As such, you won't be giving this amazing 21st-century leadership best practice and methodology of communication that is coaching a bad name.

I don't fault anyone for not knowing what effective coaching is because, after all, we don't know what we don't know. It all goes back to the leadership law of the picture: people do what they see in their leader. If you are anything like me, you probably grew up being told what to do by your parents. My stepfather was a marine and would tell us what to do, which we executed immediately or faced his wrath! Throughout school, I sat through most classes where the teacher simply pontificated to the students on the lesson plans while we sat there trying to stay awake. Then in joining the military I learned that doing what I am told by higher ranking people, especially when they yell to get it done now, is of the utmost importance, especially when lives are on the line. Then in the auto industry my manager would tell me and sell me on exactly what to do. My entire life people have been yelling, telling, or selling to get me to take action, and, lucky for me as a Gen Xer, I am fairly good at following orders, so it had worked out okay.

Think about all the parenting and management you've received in life and business. What percentage of it has been yelling, telling, or selling? If you've never officially effectively been coached before, how could you possibly know what effective coaching is? You can't.

As a result, what do we do? We perpetuate the lack of coaching when we lead through blind obedience and tell people exactly who they should be, what they should do, how we did it, how they should do it, and try to force people to be mini versions of ourselves as managers, or parents. It doesn't work because they aren't us and can't be us. If and when you are lucky enough to find someone who can be a mini version of you, just know that you won't get enough of those people to grow or even sustain your business. Coaching is not yelling, telling, or selling. Nor is coaching writing people up, firing, reprimanding, or punishing. It will take more than those tactics to retain your best employees in today's job market. It will take more than an outdated industrial era style of management to take your business, your team, your career, and your results to the next level.

A Telling Problem

There are a lot of reasons this "Telling" problem is occurring, and I will share some of them here before we dive in. The first is trainers! Trainers, I love you guys. In fact, as a young car salesperson just out of the Army, I watched my first sales training VHS tapes by a trainer named Joe Verde and was in awe. I still know those scripts like the back of my hand. That being said, trainers you need to stop confusing people by calling your training "coaching". I get it, there is a ton of competition when it comes to trainers, and you're looking for a competitive edge. Just because you call your training "coaching", doesn't make your training more valuable. When you stand in a room and tell people what to say and how to say it, this is not coaching. When people watch a video to learn something, or even take a test online about the video, this is not coaching.

Consulting is not coaching. Recently I saw a large company offering "coaching services" to car dealers. This interested me so I wanted to see what they were doing to scale up their "coaching". Turns out, they mystery shop a business online against a score card they believe are best practices. Afterward they send a one-way video communication to that business telling the business what they did wrong, what they did well, and where they can improve. This is a one-way communication, not in real time and thus does not qualify as coaching. This would fit into the consulting bucket because any conversation that is not in real time, where the process and plan to improve is pushed down from above, does not qualify as coaching.

The Selling Problem

One of the hardest things for a sales manager to do is to transform into a leader who coaches. To quote one of the titles of a favorite leadership book of mine, "What got you here won't get you there." Odds are that one of the reasons you became a sales manager was because you were an awesome salesperson. Bad news, good selling skills do not always equate to good coaching skills. In fact, the awesome sales skills that helped people like you move into management are the same skills that often hinder effective coaching.

That's right, masterful selling is preventing you from maximizing your team's full potential through coaching. The reason is because when you are selling you have an agenda. You are trying to make something specific happen by convincing someone of something. Selling is not coaching, and I will share some "Sales questions" that are often asked by sales managers early in their coaching attempts. If I told you I wasn't guilty of asking these loaded questions, I would be lying to you.

Selling question: "You know you should be (insert desired behavior here), right?"

Selling question: "So you are going to do exactly what I told you from now on then?"

Selling question: "Surely you can see how this will work, agree?"

If you are asking these questions, or similar ones, while nodding your head, then you are asking "Yes sales questions" designed to elicit the answer you want to hear. These coercive questions are for managers who want to hear the answer they desire more than the manager wants to understand reality. Attempting to coach with an agenda like this will halt coaching opportunities in their tracks, and thus prevents change and growth. When asking questions like this, your employees must give you the obvious correct answer, which is the answer you obviously want. As such, the manager using these coercive questions may get the right *answers*, but seldom the right *behavior*. Selling is not to be confused with coaching. For me, a salesperson through and through, asking questions with no agenda was the hardest behavior to change. A coach ditches the agenda and asks the following questions instead of coercing.

Coaching question: "What would be a better behavior to adopt here?"

Coaching question: "What's the best way to conduct that activity to get the results you want most?"

Coaching question: "How will your results change doing it that way?"

Letting go of the agenda and asking open-ended questions, truly trying to understand what the employee is committing to do, changes the entire dynamic of the conversation. If the trust is there for the employee to be honest, answers to the three questions above are where you start to understand the reality concerning whether the employee knows *what* to do, *how* to do it better, and sees *value* in the discussion. Understanding the reality of the employee's thoughts and beliefs is where the rubber meets the road in finding opportunities for growth. Remember all the best coaching questions begin with the words: "Who, What, When, Where, Why, and How?"

The Yelling Problem

Part of my process to begin working with a client is to do what I call a cultural assessment. I meet everyone on the team from the top down and uncover those pesky blind spots that are holding your business success back. I observe the business in action and see the senior leaders and managers interacting with their team. I get to know everyone throughout the business, their personal goals, and their unique situation, thus earning the right to coach them.

When I meet a sales manager who shares with me how frustrated they are that their people don't listen to them to the point where they think yelling is the only way to fix it, though it never does, I ask them a question. "Do you ever feel after you finish a conversation you just finished pushing a broken-down car up a hill?" They nod, laugh a bit, and cite a specific example or two where this level of frustration and exhaustion caused them to yell at someone. Here are some I've seen and heard firsthand during my cultural assessment phase.

Yelling question: "Why won't you just listen!? I told you to introduce every customer to me before they leave the showroom!"

Yelling question: "There were 10,000 dollars in bonuses available! Do you people not care about money?!"

Yelling question: "Are you happy now?! We missed our quota by two sales because you guys won't listen or come to work in order to work!"

How exhausting it is to be a manager and interact with employees in this way. At this point in your career, you've worked hard to get where you're at, and you want the best results for you and your team. Yet, all the yelling in the world doesn't even get someone to change. Hopefully, that's one of the reasons you're reading this book. You want to find better ways to communicate with your team and drive positive behavioral change that produces the results you want most. Through coaching, you will gain the tools to drive change by focusing on the actions necessary instead of focusing on results that can't change long-term behaviors. Here are some questions a masterful coach might ask instead of yelling:

Coaching question: "What is getting in the way of your introducing customers to a manager before they leave?"

Coaching question: "What would be even more motivating to you than a cash bonus?"

Coaching question: "When you don't follow through with your commitments, how would you like me to hold you responsible?"

Activity: Compare the first three selling questions and first three effective coaching questions to each other, along with the three yelling questions and second set of coaching questions to each other. Can you see the profound difference in the approaches? How would one of your employees react to each approach? What are some possible answers you might hear with each approach? Which would create the greatest opportunity for growth and why?

Are you giving Therapy or Coaching?

One of the ten motivation requirements happens to be "Valued", as in "Does my manager value me as a person, and an employee?"

Regularly listening to your employees and allowing them to express their fears, concerns, and challenges is certainly a part of coaching, yet it alone is not coaching.

I remember soon after I gained the "buy-in" for coaching from my employees and when I was first able to get them to open up to me. There was a flood of conversation. I started learning all sorts of new things about my employees' goals, desires, and challenges. I remember leaving the conversations confused. I remember asking myself, "Is coaching working?"

Soon after, in one of my first coaching conversations, I asked my coach the following question, "How do I know if coaching is working?"

He asked me a question in return, "What are you measuring?"

"Right now, I am measuring that I am consistently having the coaching conversations with each person on my team," I replied.

"Then it's working! Unless you want something else to come from these conversations. What are you hoping will come from them?" My coach questioned.

I replied, "More of the right activities and behaviors to help them achieve their goals…" and it hit me like a ton of bricks. "They aren't leaving my coaching conversations with activities."

After finishing this book on coaching, I want you to picture a mushroom cloud erupting on top of your head. This is what I experienced when learning what coaching truly was, it blew my mind to that extreme. As a special operations Sergeant in the Army, my biggest fear was losing someone on my team in combat. I didn't want to have to explain that to anyone's family, and my belief was that two things would ensure myself and my team all came home alive.

The first was technical and tactical proficiency. I believed I had to be the best at my job and that I had to be the best at using the tools available to me. For instance, I could take apart my M249 SAW, the 31-pound machine gun I carried for a year in Iraq, in less than 45 seconds. I knew every in and out of both of our loudspeaker systems, which we would use to broadcast for surrender appeals. Technical and tactical proficiency.

The second skill that I believed was crucial to our survival was leadership, so I read and studied leadership like it was the most important thing in the world. Yet, in all the leadership books I had read, I never read anything about coaching. I believe that is because coaching is relatively new to our industrial era leadership style, and most leadership books are based off leadership from that era. The reason coaching blew my mind was because it was an entirely different way of communicating. I had never seen or experienced leadership like this before, and if you haven't either, your life will be changed when adopting coaching as part of your leadership system.

To be an effective leader who coaches, part of your leadership system that must change can come from this coaching question: Who is making the commitments at the end of each coaching conversation? If you're telling them what to do, or simply listening to their woes, then you're missing out on a fundamental part of coaching. That's the part where they tell you what they are going to do, and when they are going to do it. Remember this, without an action plan, coaching is just therapy.

Coaching is NOT a Reprimand or Punishment

Each week, I lead a "Mastermind" group where twelve highly successful executives who want to be the best leader they can be for their team get together online. Our focus is on one area, and you can probably guess that it's how to be the best possible coach to make the greatest impact on the lives and results of each person on their team. One day the group wanted to discuss the barriers that prevent effective coaching from taking place, and one of the barriers that came up was trust. Not just trusting the person coaching, but also trusting that coaching was going to be positive and impactful. Gwen, one of the sales leaders in the meeting, brought up that she had some new people on her team and wanted to begin coaching them immediately. We discussed some of the things she would need to do in order to earn the right to coach her people.

Gwen would have to learn their expectations for coaching. That's right, I said *learn their* expectations, not *set her* expectations. Some of the questions Gwen decided to ask, as a result of our Mastermind discussion, were the following:

- What does coaching mean to you?
- How would you like to be coached?
- What would make coaching positive and impactful for you?
- If you could select the topic of each coaching conversation, what challenges or obstacles would you like coaching to address?
- How frequently would you like to sit down with your manager and receive coaching?
- How long would you like the conversations to last?
- What concerns do you have about coaching?
- What career goals would you like coaching to help you achieve?

You see, Gwen and the other leaders in the Mastermind created a way to learn their direct reports' expectations about coaching. In reality, they were learning how each person on the team wanted to be developed, communicated with, and led.

The following week Gwen had an interesting and unforgettable story to tell. One of her new team members who had answered those questions had a prior manager who used to "coach" them. The version of coaching this person described was far more like being yelled at, degraded, and devalued by a drill sergeant. That old manager had called what they did with the employee "coaching". As a result, this employee was terrified of the word "coaching". Only after learning the employee's expectations and what coaching meant to them, and what would make it valuable for them, did Gwen earn the right to coach them. This created trust by redefining the definition of coaching for Gwen's new employee. Gwen's new employee learned that coaching is not discipline or reprimand.

I want to share one last visual as we transition from what coaching is not, to what coaching is. Picture in your mind's eye a large closed off room with a white tile floor. The room is empty except for a 2 foot by 2 foot X painted in the middle of the floor, and a bunny rabbit. You can decide what color the rabbit is, I'll leave that up to you, just make sure it's cute and cuddly. Now imagine your goal is to get the bunny rabbit to stand on the X on the floor in the middle of the room.

You have two ways you can go about doing it. You can smack the bunny rabbit with a stick and see where he ends up, poor bunny. Or you can lay a carrot on the X and see what happens. Which would you pick? I hope you don't enjoy hitting cute, defenseless bunnies with sticks and instead chose the carrot! At the end of the day, you can reprimand an employee, making them feel fear and pain. They'll move. They may not move in the direction you want them to go; heck, they may move right out of your business and into a better leader's care. Or you can find out what they want most, their carrot, and watch them effortlessly go there. There is enough fear and pain in the world that people don't need their managers creating more of it. Instead, motivate your people through excitement by helping them get what they want. We'll talk more about that in the next section on what coaching is.

To recap what coaching isn't, let's revisit the Raven Paradox: all things that are training, consulting, therapy, reprimand, telling, selling, yelling, coercing, convincing, screaming, degrading, insulting, pushing, forcing, or smacking with a stick, are NOT coaching.

Chapter 3

Understand what Coaching IS

Coaching is many things, the first being a gift you give your people. Do you agree with me that time is our most precious resource and something you can never get back? If so, then by investing your time in others, you are giving them one of the greatest gifts of all. The gift of your life!

Think about it like this: a gift is always for the person who is receiving that gift. What kind of gifts do people like most? The answer is simple: a gift that they want most! To that end, the receiver of coaching, or coachee as I often call them, gets to choose the objective of the conversation. The coachee gets to pick the topic or topics to receive coaching on, with the intent to help them achieve their desired outcome. The coachee determines exactly what they want to take away and change as a result of the coaching conversation. As such, there is always a guaranteed value add because they are getting the gift they want. I believe so vehemently in this, and my conviction is so strong, that if you can find me a single effective coaching conversation where value wasn't added for the coachee, reach out to me and explain it. If you can prove me wrong, I will refund you 100% of whatever you paid to get this book! Heck, I will buy you a plane ticket, fly you to my home in St. Louis, and smoke you some of the best BBQ you've ever had in my big green egg, and we can talk about it.

In fact, coaching is such a value add that the simple act of giving coaching to someone may result in extreme pay increases for both parties, less stress, promotions, huge positive life changes for multiple parties, or even many other unintentional positive results.

Case in point, it was a hot summer day in August of 2014 A.C. (after coaching). I had successfully integrated coaching into my leadership routine at my dealership, and it was having a profound impact. I remember celebrating that we hadn't lost an employee on our sales team in months. And I was ready for a new challenge. I was beginning to wonder, "Does coaching only work on my employees, or do I have the ability to coach people who don't work for me?" I started brainstorming about who I could reach out to and offer some coaching.

The next day, as if God himself heard my question and gave me an answer, Dave Fultz, the CEO of DriveCentric CRM software walked into my dealership. DriveCentric was a local start-up company that, at the time, was generating a couple million dollars a year in recurring revenue. Dave had sold our dealership their software a year or two prior and was visiting the local dealerships trying to retain his customers. He was in his early forties, a high strung and intense guy who had a lot of experience as a senior leader at dealerships and spent a few years as a finance department consultant for dealerships throughout the Midwest region. Dave had a team of people in St. Louis and Indiana and wanted to ensure his company's success so they could feed their families. Also, Dave as an entrepreneur had spent his life savings investing in the development of his software. He had risked everything to get where he was, and it was a precarious situation at best.

As soon as he walked in, I could see that he was having a rough day and seemed pretty stressed about something. After greeting him and making a little small talk I asked him, "Dave, you seem a little stressed out, what's going on?"

He replied anxiously, "Nothing I want to trouble you with, but thanks for asking."

Not wanting to let an opportunity to help him slip through my grasp, I asked him to join me in one of the finance offices so that we could get some privacy and I could build confidence and trust. "Dave, I really enjoy using your software, and I want to continue to use your software. Not to mention, the owner of my company values my opinion, so if you're having an issue, I would be happy to go to bat for you. Also, if it's something completely different, I would be honored to discuss your challenge in strict confidence, and maybe I could even help you somehow."

Dave relaxed and let loose, "Okay, here's the problem. I'm having a hard time keeping clients happy. It seems like no matter what I do, they get frustrated with their employees and want to give up on the CRM."

I could sense the gravity of the situation, and I wanted to ensure we discovered his desired objective from this coaching conversation. "Dave, I want for you to be able to retain your clients, and for you to be stress free knowing they're sticking with you long term. If you left this conversation with some clarity and a better plan on how to retain your clients, or better make them happy, would that be valuable for you, or is there something even more important we should focus on?"

Dave wore his heart on his sleeve and instantly became ecstatic, "YES! That."

"Who are your clients?" I asked.

"The dealer principal, the owner." Dave replied.

I needed to know more, "What are the frustrations they share with you?"

"You know with software there are always going to be little glitches. On top of that, it seems like everyone wants us to personalize the software for them. We only have so much development time, and the dealers think we can make anything, anytime. I explain the vision to them, then they want me to talk to their managers who don't really get what we're trying to create. It's really frustrating," Dave elaborated.

The details Dave shared pointed to a bigger overarching issue than a single client challenge, and I had to explore this further. "If the dealer is frustrated, what reason are they giving you when they want you to talk to their managers?"

Dave thought about it for a moment and replied, "I think it's because their managers can explain the issues they're having better than the owner."

"Interesting," I thought out loud, remembering all the times Dave's people had come and gone from my dealership, there to see the owners. I went on, "Is that an assumption, or did they tell you that?"

"They told me that." Dave replied.

"Can you walk me through the specific conversation you had the last time an issue like this arose?" I questioned.

Without hesitation Dave replied, "Okay, so the other day one of our clients called me and said," he changed his facial expression and voice to mimic the angry client: "Dave, you need to do something about the tiles on the home screen. It doesn't have a few of the features X salesperson and Y manager want. You need to address this right away."

"And how did you respond?" I probed deeper, listening intently.

"I said, look, DriveCentric is NOT just any old CRM, we have a vision and we know the direction we're taking this thing and the next version of DriveCentric will eliminate the tiles anyhow and be 1000% more useful. Let me build the next version instead of trying to put band-aids on the old one…"

I asked, "What did the dealer do next?"

"His exact words. Here, just call Stan the manager, I'm tired of hearing about it." Dave quoted the dealer.

I thought I was onto something and had potentially uncovered the missing puzzle piece and I wanted to verify that, "Dave, who are your clients?"

"I already told you, the dealer," Dave stated, appearing slightly bewildered that I asked him the same question I had earlier.

I challenged his statement with another question, "What makes you say the dealer is the client?"

Pulling from his past experience as a dealership consultant and GM, he began to get more animated and said, "Because they're the ones that write the check!"

I wanted to challenge his belief, "How much are the dealers using your software?"

"Not very much, I'm pretty sure of that," he returned.

"And what makes them stop writing a check?" I asked.

"If they're not happy," Dave answered immediately.

"What makes them not happy?" I dug in.

Dave responded hesitantly, "Ummm, their employees nagging them, complaining to them about their issues with the system or ideas they want us to develop for them, or their users not using the software."

Now it was time to verify this was a missing puzzle piece, or even better, help him arrive at a new level of understanding, "Dave, again I ask you, WHO are your clients?" I accentuated the WHO to give him a clue.

I wanted Dave to realize in all his efforts to appease the dealer, if he wasn't satisfying the actual users of the software, somehow, some way, he could never maximize his potential or relieve his stress because the "check writers" would only tolerate so many complaints from their employees for so long.

Dave thought about it, and his face turned slightly red. "I'm not sure where you're going with this, but PLEASE TELL ME," he pleaded.

"If the dealer is the customer, and they don't really use the software in their role, then why do they keep passing you onto their employees to discuss issues with it?" I wasn't quite ready to give in to his pleas.

He sat back in his chair, squinted his eyes a bit and rested his fist on his chin making a pose resembling the thinking man statue, "Are you saying I need to treat all the users like they're the customer?"

I chuckled a bit at his animated reactions to my questions and helped him fill in the rest of the missing puzzle pieces, "I can't know

Chapter 3: Understand what Coaching IS

for sure because I haven't asked them... Could it be possible that your dealers are only giving into the frustration the managers and or other front line users are expressing to them about the software?"

"Wow, I never looked at it like that before. I have a lot to think about," Dave said, still deep in thought.

I wanted to see if Dave was already formulating a plan to address his greatest challenge, "If you had to do it right now, how would you go about addressing that issue?"

Dave sighed, "I have no idea, but there's got to be some way to support all the users of DriveCentric... Sean, I can't thank you enough for this conversation. I have work to do."

Before I could wrap up the coaching convo by co-creating an action plan, or confirming the value of the conversation, Dave grabbed his briefcase and started to make a beeline toward the door. I felt like something was missing so I threw one last Hail Mary question at him, "When do you want me to reach out to see what you come up with?"

He simply looked back and smiled, replying, "I'll be in touch."

About two weeks had passed by, and I was still working up the courage to call Dave. All of a sudden my phone rang and it was an unknown number. I picked up.

The caller didn't hesitate, "Sean, it's Dave, I am calling to thank you for our conversation."

"Oh! Hey, Dave, you're welcome, it was an honor to sit down and give you some coaching." I stated.

"Some what?" Dave asked.

I then realized I never explained to Dave that I was actively following my process to give him some guaranteed value through coaching, "Never mind that! May I ask what specific impact our conversation had for you?" I asked.

"Well, I changed the entire direction of my company and how we serve our clients because of that conversation. I'm not exaggerating when I say it was the best business conversation I've had in a couple years. I told my business partners how you helped me get the muck out of my eyes. I'd like to have talks like that again some time, if you'd be willing. Also, how can I thank you?" he asked sincerely.

"It's funny you should ask. I have recently decided I want to be a coach, and I've already proven the impact coaching has at my dealership. That being said, if I am to even think about doing it full time, I need to prove to myself that I can coach people other than my employees. Make sense?" I asked.

"You want to do what? I'm not sure what you mean when you say you want to coach," Dave replied.

I chuckled, thinking about how I was in his shoes about coaching just a year before. "Coaching is what I gave you in the conversation we had the other day. Imagine if conversations like we had, along with the measurable success that came from them, were duplicated regularly, over and over for you and each person on your team? What would that mean for you and your company?" I asked open-endedly.

"It would mean everything," Dave replied without hesitation.

I asked him what my soul had been burning to ask him since the moment I was blessed enough to be given the opportunity to coach him. "If it's okay with you, I would like to come meet with your team, explain to you and to them what coaching is, and then see if they would like to sign up for my program. Would you allow me to meet

Chapter 3: Understand what Coaching IS

with everyone at your headquarters?" I held my breath for what seemed an eternity but was probably less than two seconds.

"Let's do it," Dave said.

You see, coaching is a guaranteed value add for others. I know the word "guarantee" may come across a little watered down from someone in the auto industry! Jokes aside, effective coaching is always a value add, because, like I said, coaching is a gift you are giving to others. It's what you know they want, and you are always giving them a missing puzzle piece they didn't have.

Here is my long and thorough definition of effective coaching: coaching is when a leader constantly invests time and energy in someone to develop in the area the coachee wants to grow most, in the best way for that person. It starts by first discovering what they want, then asking them questions which allow the coachee to self-discover areas of opportunity for improvement. The leader then sheds light on their blind spots, challenging the employee's limiting beliefs with powerful questions. The coach empowers the coachee to create the solution to their opportunity while collaborating around the plan's effectiveness and trusting the coachee to leverage their own individual personal strengths to execute on the solution. All of this is done while supporting them throughout the process of growth until measurable new behaviors and/or results have occurred, and then maintaining the development with the cycle of continuous improvement.

Now, let's identify elements of effective coaching, ensuring that each coaching convo guarantees value for your coachee, and guaranteeing people you work with will look forward to your coaching conversations. Your desire to start coaching will go through the roof because you will understand how coaching is the one true method to ensure that business and career growth persists in a cycle of continuous improvement.

Chapter 4

Set Your GPS

Imagine you and your family decide to go on vacation, but you don't plan where you want to go at all. You just get in your car and start driving. When do you need to stop and eat? Where will you end up? Did you pack the right stuff for where you will end up? Do you have enough money for the vacation? How long before your family members start questioning, where are we going and when will we be there? How long before they start nagging you to give them an ETA? Let's say you go to the airport. Now you're booking a flight at the last minute which means it's costing you a premium, or worse, you can't get tickets at all! There are great odds that you end up somewhere much less desirable, taking you much longer to arrive, and at a significantly greater cost than if you had simply chosen your destination first.

Obviously, taking a vacation like this sounds silly, right? Yet, people do this in business all the time! Someone decides to start selling cars, or real estate, or office equipment, or medical supplies to "Try it out and see what happens". They don't have a clear vision for success, nor are their goals aligned to what they want most. They start doing the "what" with no clear understanding of the "why", "how", or "where" they want to go. As a result, bad habits become part of how they do business. These habits, both good and bad, shape their results both good and bad, and their results shape their values and beliefs. Ultimately, these values, beliefs, and results take you to your destination. Once they realize the destination is not somewhere they want to be, they start looking for the next best thing: a new job! Once they end up finding it, they start an aimless career path again. This often occurs most when people are merely selling for the money.

Set Your G.P.S. – Goals, Purpose, and Significance (But Not in that Order!)

Instead of allowing our people to fall into this pitfall, we need to help them achieve greatness by starting with the end in mind. First, clearly define the purpose, learn the reason that purpose is significant to them, then work backward to set goals that will ensure they are moving toward their vision for success.

Purpose

While first visiting a Mazda dealership in Kentucky, I attended a month-end sales meeting where the General Manager yelled at his team. "There were ten thousand dollars in bonuses available to you last month. None of you even tried to get them! Do you not care about money?"

I remember thinking, "I wonder if this GM knows what they *do* care about?"

It's interesting when you talk to salespeople in almost any industry about the reasons they are in commissioned sales. When asked, "Why do you do what you do?" The knee-jerk response is often, "For the money". Of course, money is one of the chief reasons we go to work in the first place. It is also a motivator for most salespeople, to some degree, especially for those of us that have been broke before! While a definite motivator, money is not the best *purpose*.

I'd argue that if sales managers helped their people by focusing less on the commission check and more on a deeper purpose, this would ultimately yield more money. Sound unbelievable? Let's think this through.

Managers, here are three problems with having salespeople selling just for the money. Below each problem is a list of symptoms to help you diagnose if you have salespeople suffering from a money purpose.

1. Money is the Result of Actions, Behaviors, Messaging and Attitude

Money is not the reason a salesperson gets paid. There is a direct link between purpose and the actions, reactions, and attitudes which replicate the result time after time. Can money be that purpose? No. Quite the opposite. Think about an elated customer interaction that ends in a profitable sale. It's almost always a situation where the buyer feels like they are winning because the salesperson did a great job when building value in themselves and their product. They likely did that while holding true to your processes and selling best practices.

On the contrary, when salespeople focus only on the money they need to make, the "sale" is about the company and the salesperson, not the customer. Most customers sniff this out, and if you are lucky enough to sell them once, they won't be back to see you again.

Symptoms: Top-earning salespeople at your store may have low customer satisfaction. Sales are transactional. You see little to no repeat or referral business. You are often dealing with customer complaints. People want to return their car or have excessive buyer's remorse. Customers leave saying "I need to think it over" or "It just doesn't feel right".

A great coaching question managers can start asking salespeople deals with the initial customer interactions. "How do you plan on creating a customer for life with this client?"

Salespeople can ask their customers the following question, "How can I exceed your expectations and earn you as a customer for life today?"

2. Money Gains Have Very Real Diminishing Returns on Motivation

Did you know every state has a money happiness threshold? That is the point at which more money does not create more happiness. This is the margin for diminishing returns when it comes to income. Though not every person or household has this same threshold, money is a quenchable thirst that, once sated, may cause lack of motivation and desire to achieve.

Symptoms: Salespeople on your team are on an every-other-month roller coaster ride. Salespeople come out swinging, start off strong, then sales taper off the rest of the month. Lackluster motivation from salespeople once they hit their internal money benchmark. You see people on your team kicking back and relaxing after hitting their goal. Salespeople who seem content, even though they aren't top producers making big money.

Coaching questions managers can ask their salespeople to find something other than money to motivate them are: "Other than money, what else motivates you?" and "If you did have all the money in the world, what would you do with it?"

I was coaching a salesperson named Lewis who was frustrating his manager because he was certain Lewis could be a top producer, but just didn't seem motivated. The manager had written him off as lazy. Looking at Lewis, though, I could tell from the condition he was in that he probably spent a couple of hours every day working out. That's not the sign of a lazy man! A conversation with Lewis revealed that money was not a motivator for him; he didn't really need it. In fact, he was working at the dealership just so he'd have something to do with his days.

I immediately began to ask him more questions, trying to uncover what he was passionate about. It turned out he'd lost four immediate family members to cancer and participated in runs and other fundraising events for cancer research. Now we were getting somewhere. I asked him if he sold more cars what could he do with the money he didn't need. He lit up when he realized he could donate the money to the cancer research. When we ended the coaching session, he had a plan to donate a portion of every car sale to cancer research and to advertise that was what he was doing. By fulfilling his passion and aligning his job with his life's purpose, his sales went through the roof!

3. Commission Structures Can and Will Change

A myriad of uncontrollable factors can impact your salespeople when it comes to income. Pay plans change, factory spiffs can be dropped, inventory costs fluctuate, market conditions vary (we saw a lot of this in 2020), and competition may arise. If money is their sole purpose and one of these uncontrollable changes occur, your salesperson is going to be down in the dumps. They will feel like a victim instead of someone in charge of their own destiny, which is no way to enjoy a career.

If you, as a manager, focus on a deeper reason for doing their job than money, when bad things happen to the compensation structure that we can't always control, it will be like water off a duck's back. In turn, if your salespeople have a greater reason, working is no longer linked to the pay plan. Thus, they won't feel as much of a sting.

Symptoms: Salespeople getting a bad attitude when they have a minimum commission. When incentives change or the factory changes spiffs there is doom and gloom in the air. Commissioned salespeople asking for a raise, threatening to quit, or even quitting for more money elsewhere.

Managers can ask their employees the following coaching question, "What impact do your results have on the rest of the company?" and "Are you open to sitting down and trying to uncover a greater reason for what we do each day?"

Managers, hopefully, you can now see the problems associated with selling just for the money. You might even recognize some of these symptoms in yourself.

On the other hand, if you're still convinced that the hunger for higher commissions is the best motivator, then I challenge you to think about your long-term selling strategy. How will your dealership compensate as customers can simply buy from websites where cars are dropped in their driveways? How will you build your dealership after a massive product recall? Chasing the dollar is not a sustainable, long-term plan.

As a sales manager, when I focused on selling more units and making more gross I did well and so did my salespeople. Yet, only after realizing my greater purpose, to impact the lives of as many professionals across the country as I could and leave a legacy of success and knowledge in all the lives I am blessed enough to touch, have I started to move toward my potential. Only by helping each of my salespeople discover their greater purpose did we reach extreme success as a team, setting those first time regional records. Upgrading the reason you do what you do for yourself and your employees isn't as difficult as you may think! It just takes a few questions with each individual to really help them identify their better purpose.

Step 1. Discover Individual Purpose

Ask yourself, and each member of your sales team, the following questions:

- If you had unlimited money, what would you do with it?
- Define your brand for me. What do you want to be remembered for by your family, friends, and peers? How do you want your customers to remember you?

- What would it mean to you to accomplish your financial goals working here? How would you feel? Why would that be important?
- Why is accomplishing this financial success important to you?
- Imagine you're 90 years old and your local newspaper writes an article about your career, what do you want it to say?
- If your next customer tweeted about your level of service and every single buyer in our market would read it, what would you want to be known for?
- If your sales team wrote a biography about you, what would you want to be remembered for in your book?

Step 2: Build a Team Purpose

Next, think about your team and ask yourself and/or them these questions:

- What can you and your team strive for as a group next year?
- What group reward or recognition would be most impactful to your team and what could everyone do to earn it?
- Thinking big, what can you do to align the entire team behind a common cause?

Step 3: Reinforce the Purpose

It will take long-term commitment to ensure this becomes the new norm for each employee and the team as a whole. Do so with the following questions:

- Your purpose is "X." Did you fulfill that purpose with that last customer engagement?
- How do you feel about your efforts toward your purpose today?
- What are you doing to consistently live out your values and fulfill the deeper reason for what you do?
- How is working toward your new purpose more rewarding?

By asking the questions above you may find some pretty amazing reasons your employees get out of bed in the morning. To list a few that I have heard: "I want to be able to take care of my single mother." "I want to better take care of my disabled child." "I want my kids to be happy." "I want to do so well for my customers, that they never think of going to anyone but me for their purchase." "If we can hit X Goal as a team, we will set records never before accomplished in our dealership or market." "I want to help people with the same credit and financial challenges I had get what they want." "I want to live stress-free knowing I have a sustainable career that continues to grow due to my customer retention." "I want to be known as the most professional and skilled salesperson my company has ever had." "I want to leave seven figures to my family when I pass."

"I want to retire at the age of 55 and travel the world with my wife of 35 years." "I want to get my girlfriend an engagement ring and then the wedding of her dreams." "I want to be the first one in my family to pay for my kids' college education." "I want to be stress free knowing I am investing in a great nest egg for retirement." "I want to be respected throughout the organization as the most professional and knowledgeable salesperson here." "I want to promote everyone on my team and never have to hire from outside." "I want my company to be the best place to work in my city."

Now you have uncovered a better, deeper purpose for each of your team members that will actually drive results and enhance your employees' selling experience as well as your customers' buying experience. You may begin to notice a little more hop in your employees' steps as they interact with customers. Your buyers may seem a little happier as they have a better reason to spend their money with you instead of your competitors.

Once reinforcing the purpose for each salesperson becomes a habit, you may notice the morale of your salespeople improve. Regardless of market conditions and other non-controllable challenges, they still seem inspired. Your buyers will remember the purchase and will be more apt to come back again or offer referrals to family and friends when asked. Your reputation both with company surveys, on the street, and online will likely start to improve. Their reason isn't all about the money anymore; it's stronger and more meaningful.

Any time you need to hold someone responsible, or generate buy-in around a new initiative, you will start off by bringing up the reason you uncovered here. We'll discuss that more later.

Do yourself, your employees, and your entire industry a favor and help everyone find a purpose. Everyone needs a better reason for selling that is less fickle than cash. Link the purpose to the behaviors that lead to success with a reason for selling even more unquenchable than the thirst for money. In doing so, you can massively increase your own production and that of every single member of your sales team. Your team will also feel a greater reward for the work they do. I wish you the best in helping each salesperson on your team find this better reason than money in what they do!

One of the greatest things about coaching people toward their purpose is that it gives a leader the ability to develop and add value to any person of any age, tenure, experience level, and job role on their team. Managers are generally only comfortable training and developing people in job roles that they've specialized in now or in the past. On the other hand, a leader who coaches can and will leverage coaching to great effect for anyone on the team, regardless of whether they know their role or not.

The coaching story below illustrates that fact for several reasons. First, Tony, the gentleman in this story, has far more experience and skills running entire service departments than myself. Second, Tony is 25 years my senior in age. Third, no matter someone's age, skill level, or tenure, everyone wants more of or less of something. If a coach uses the right approach, he or she can change and improve the lives of everyone around them!

After passing through the quiet Nissan service department, I sat down with the white-haired service director in his small octagonal shaped office. His window overlooked the service drive. He had a crisply starched button up shirt, pressed pants, and nice dress shoes.

His office looked impeccably organized, and I could tell he was very deliberate in all his activities. He was an experienced, mentally sharp, technically savvy service leader who had just been hired back by the dealership after a five-year hiatus. During his break, he was the chief of a fire department, and a locally elected government official. He was inheriting a service department that had extremely low customer retention, customer experience survey scores (known as CSI), and had nowhere to go but up regarding sales. This is the GPS coaching conversation that ensued.

"It's great to meet you, Tony. I've heard great things about you from the owner of the company who is excited you're back on the team!" I said enthusiastically while giving the service director a firm handshake.

He smiled and with a light New Jersey accent replied, "It's good meeting you as well."

"What do you already know about what I do for your company?" I asked the shrewd and confident looking service director.

He thought for a moment, and a curious look came across his face, "Only that you come in and give 1-on-1's to some of the managers and salespeople. And that our dealership principal and the prior service manager say they get a lot out of working with you. What exactly do you do?"

"Well, that's nice of them. Since this is our first conversation, I would like to learn about your vision for success, some of your short term, mid-range, and long term goals, and finally your expectations around coaching." I continued, "Basically, the root word meaning of the word 'coach' means to take people where you want to go. To that point, I believe my only job is to know where you want to go in your business and your life, and to help you move toward that destination. That's why your vision for success is so important to this process, and in our working together. Also, I can't coach with you the same way I would coach with Michael, Roy, Gilbert, or Steve. Coaching is always tailored for the individual, so I need to learn how you like to receive coaching so that I can ensure it's best for you." I wrapped up with permission to continue. "May I start off by asking you some questions to get clarity on your vision for success?" I asked.

"Interesting, go right ahead." he replied thoughtfully.

I locked eyes with the manager to ask him a very deep question, "Imagine for a moment that there are no obstacles to your version of success, most anything's possible, and you can write your own destiny. What would success in both work and your personal life look like for you over the next three years?"

Clutching my digital notebook and stylus, I prepared to furiously take notes.

"Wow. That's a big question. Well, I will humbly say that my entire career I've had a lot of success. Everything from setting records for multiple service departments in large dealer groups, to making a great living, and honorably helping the people that work with me in my service departments succeed in their careers. I love seeing people grow and move up, and a lot of people that have worked for me over the years are top producers or are running their own dealerships." He paused to think.

I could tell this man was humble, deliberate, authentic, and cared about his people. I could also tell that he was deciding if he could yet trust me. "Before you say anything else, let me promise that anything we talk about is in confidence. I will not share anything we discuss without your permission."

He smiled, "Okay, that's good to know. I appreciate that."

I smiled back, "Also, you can trust me. I used to be a car salesman."

We both burst out in laughter.

He replied, "Point taken!" With a grin and continued.

"Okay, I feel that a lot of my success came from me rolling my sleeves up, getting in the trenches, leading by example, and doing the work myself. Which has worked great for me my entire life but…" he paused.

It seemed like he was ready to succeed another way, "But what?"

"But that means I have to work a lot of hours, and to get the results I know we can get I will have to continue living at the dealership. And I'm a hard worker. I don't want you to get the idea I'm not willing to work." He pondered his next thoughts.

"What part of your vision for success could your working to succeed the way you have in the past get in the way of?" I asked curiously.

"That's just it. My entire life I've put my job, my teams, and the businesses I've worked for ahead of my wife. She's been great about it, has supported me the entire time, never really complained, and I want to give back to her," he proclaimed with a fire in his eyes.

I believe a manager starts a fire under people, whereas a leader starts a fire *within* people. That's one of the results I love most about the G.P.S. conversation—its impact on individuals' motivation.

I now knew this sharp leader was a loving husband and appreciated the thought he had arrived at, "Then in this vision for success, what would you be doing more or less of?"

"To answer your question, if anything were possible, three years from now I would be spending evenings with Lisa, actually taking my day off, spending it with Lisa. I'd be going on several vacations a year, with Lisa. We would be doing more with our kids and our grandkids. But I don't know how that would be possible with work." The light in his eyes started to dwindle.

I had to remind him of the goal of our conversation today, "Remember, you're not allowed to be a critic, yet! Right now, anything's possible! So, in this vision, you're spending more time with your wife, taking your day off. What else would success look like for you?"

He smiled warmly, "Okay, in that case, regardless of if I was at the dealership or not, we would be getting the same top performing results. I would be able to leave work, trusting that everyone on my team would know what to do, when to do it, and how to do it."

"What would that mean for you?" I asked.

He replied immediately, "It would mean peace of mind. I could truly be present with my wife and give her all my focus and attention."

"Now we're getting somewhere, and I'm going to talk about your vision for success again in the present tense. Let's make sure nothing's missing from it! You've turned this into a high functioning service department, your team's mastered all the right things, and you trust them implicitly. You're taking your nights off, your days off, and you're able to unplug and be with your wife and kids when you're outside the dealership both mentally and physically. Is anything missing we should add?"

"No, that would be my vision for success!" he stated.

I asked Tony, "How do you feel about it?"

"It sounds amazing."

"Okay, now you can be the critic!" I grinned. "What could get in the way of this vision becoming a reality?"

Tony joked, "That's just it. I guess my first thought is, if I make the team that good, what would they need me for?" He chuckled.

Knowing there's always a bit of truth to every joke, I asked him a coaching question to try and challenge him around that limiting belief, "In your career, how many managers have you met that have been fired for making a bunch of the people on their team awesome top performers?"

"Never once," he replied. "Good point! That's what a manager's job is."

"Okay, then! For this vision to become a reality, what short-term, mid-range and long-term goals will you need to achieve?" I asked.

"Well, first I will need to start great mentoring relationships with my assistant manager and my parts manager. If I don't start mentoring them, pouring into them, then none of this will be possible. In fact, I'll need to stop doing everything myself, or, at the very least, show them what I'm doing while I'm doing it." He had set his first short-term goal.

"Wonderful goal!" I exclaimed while jotting down some more notes before asking, "What about mid-range, let's say six to eighteen months?"

Chapter 4: Set Your GPS

"I think building an in-house call center would be important, because then we'd be able to do outbound calls to drive up business and make sure every customer gets handled properly before they even visit the dealership." He added it to his goals list.

"What else?" I asked.

"I think that's good for mid-range goals," he concluded.

"What about your vacations and time off with your wife? What goals focused on that will you commit to accomplishing within the next six to eighteen months?" As his coach, I wasn't about to let him off the hook for that.

He laughed, "You got me! That's the whole point of this vision." He continued, "After six months we will be hitting our goals. I will be leaving when the office closes while getting everything done. And at eighteen months, I will be taking my days off. And in the short term, I will schedule my first vacation with Lisa."

"And what can I do to support you in accomplishing these goals?" I asked thoughtfully.

"Hold me accountable. Continue coaching with me. And help me build my business development call center." He told me straightforwardly.

"Is that it?" I asked with a grin.

We laughed together.

Over the next eighteen months, Tony, myself and one of my service department specialized coaches poured into his managers and his service advisors. Together we recruited, staffed, and trained his call center. We focused on employee motivation and staffing. With the support of Car Motivators coaching, Tony and his team were able to eliminate low surveys, hire and retain service technicians, improve shop capacity, and began setting first time regional records for customer experience, customer retention, and dealership profit in service.

But wait, there's more! The next big coaching convo with Tony led to an even bigger growth mindset. Once Tony started spending more time with his wife, he realized that he also needed to make more money to fund the extra time and experiences they were enjoying together, while letting his wife retire. This led to his desiring to grow his career to an entirely new level of success, one that he had never achieved before. Tony decided that either becoming a fixed ops director for multiple stores in the dealer group or learning the sales side of the business and becoming a General Manager who would oversee the entire dealership was the next stage in his career.

We've since been coaching on that, and as a result he has grown his success to GM level, and the owner of his business has made a commitment to give him the store at the end of the year that this book is being written. The plan to get there has increased sales because by learning about the sales side of the business, he's been able to help sales grow. It's created more team cohesion, and the managers on the sales side want to learn from and be mentored by him. As the dealership managers have growth under Tony's leadership, their departments' results have drastically improved. With the improved management from his leadership, the dealership owners have more time to focus on building their business across the board.

One of the most beautiful parts of this entire outcome: Tony's motivation and passion for wanting to spend more quality time with his wife was the fuel for this. The powerful lesson is that people aren't motivated by what the business wants them to do. They are motivated by what the business can do for their life. When you focus on that, you can uncover and create superhuman motivation, and drive positive change. Even the most tenured, experienced, skilled leaders at the tail end of their career still want more or less of something. A leader who coaches can find out what that is and help them move toward that vision. That's how a leader who can coach, regardless of age and experience, can add value to anyone. Moreover, that's the power of coaching someone on their purpose.

Significance

Now that we have discussed purpose in depth, let's talk about significance. Significance is the reason their vision for success matters in the first place. Understanding the significance behind the purpose is crucial for your ability to move that person toward what they want most, in a way that is real and relevant to their core values. Without understanding the significance, you may not be able to help the individual you're trying to help achieve their vision.

For example, as a result of my upbringing, my personal desire for the satisfaction that comes from consistent hard work and dedication is only rivaled by my aversion to doing things the "easy way" and taking "shortcuts". If someone were trying to help me achieve more success in less time yet trying to do it in a way that I perceive as a "get rich quick scheme," it would be a disqualifier for me. Even if the result was the same, or even better, to me the value that comes from achieving something I've worked hard on, far outtrumps the result itself if that result came too easily.

Once, I allowed someone on my team who did not share these values, and in fact outright opposed them. Throughout their entire tenure with my people development company, Car Motivators, Inc., I felt like everything they did was attempting to "get rich quick". It was like someone trying out for a professional baseball team, swinging for the fences hoping to hit a home run, without putting in the dedication and practice it takes to earn the right to hit a home run in the major leagues. To succeed in the people development business in a very competitive industry, it takes a commitment to personal growth, massive effort to generate relationships with potential clients, and a never-ending search to add value for our clients. He didn't see it that way and wanted to get rich quick. We ultimately had to part ways as friends. Even though this person wanted the same results for my company as me, the means by which each of us wanted to get there differed.

What if they're not coachable?

One of the fantastic leaders I serve, a highly motivated and skilled General Sales Manager who leads one of the best sales teams in Florida, reached out to me recently, asking for some content on what makes someone coachable. Not unlike many leaders, I used to label people "coachable" or "not coachable". My process for deciding so looked like this:

Step 1. Tell them what to do.

Step 2. Tell them how to do it.

Step 3. Expect they do it.

In reality, since this is not coaching, it wasn't fair for me to label anyone not coachable. Since we have already detailed what coaching is and what coaching is not, let's assume the coach has read that and the rest of the book's chapters. Let's take into account that the coach is effectively leveraging the tools provided. Proper coaching does not mean that every coaching conversation creates a permanent change in behavior or mindset. Does that mean these people aren't coachable?

Before exploring this further, I want to point out that how each person wants to receive coaching is different and subjective. Each coach's style also varies. Since everyone wants more of something, people who want something are likely to try and get it. The question should change from, are they coachable to "Are they coachable by me?" If the styles don't match, that can create an issue. If the coach isn't willing to coach the employee on what the employee wants, it can generate a coachability issue. Problems like this are more about "compatibility" than "coachability".

Since coaching is a gift from the coach and a present to be received for the coachee, let's discuss both sides so that you as a leader can determine who you should and shouldn't invest in. Also, people receiving coaching can ask themselves some tough questions and be introspective enough to identify if they are the problem.

When I was first building my coaching business, I learned that every person in the service industry needs what speaker and coach Michael Port calls a "red velvet rope" policy in his book *Book Yourself Solid*. He compares this to the red velvet rope at the entrance to a high-end nightclub where they only let the people they desire into the party. As such, I decided to create my red velvet rope and decided I would only coach people that have the following traits:

1. Optimistic can-do attitude
2. Positive outlook
3. Faith-based beliefs
4. Enjoys continuous self-improvement
5. Enjoys growth
6. Problem solvers
7. Family values
8. Enjoys helping others
9. Authentic
10. Driven and committed
11. Takes ownership
12. Successful and goal-oriented
13. Open, honest, willing to be vulnerable
14. Follow up habits
15. Values two-way discussion

I next defined people's traits I would want to avoid coaching with like the plague and came up with this list:

1. Know-it-all
2. Not willing to listen
3. Refuses to implement their own ideas
4. Repeat cancellations
5. Unreliability
6. Not mindful of others' time
7. No ambition
8. No empathy or care for others
9. Eternal unwarranted negativity

10. Unwilling to improve
11. Already "perfect"
12. Questionable ethics
13. Poor morals and values
14. Lack of trust
15. Puts money over the value of their people

Your list may be similar to mine, or it may be completely different. What matters is understanding that many of these traits can be uncovered during the initial expectation learning conversation. Others present themselves later as you go through the coaching process. For instance, part of my coaching process is to co-create an action plan. The objective is that the coachee tells you what they are going to do. Suppose the person receiving coaching commits to calling ten prospects a day and doesn't. In that case, this could mean they possess the negative traits on my list, #3 refuses to implement their own ideas, and #5 unreliability. At first glance, it's easy to make this assumption, and that's what most managers do. However, it's not necessarily the case. What else might be possible? Did they run out of prospects to call? Did they try it thirty times and got poor results, so they stopped? Did something else more pressing take up the time in their routine?

A coach needs to be fair when helping people grow and understand that change and growth almost always require discomfort, and often failure. You have to support your coachee and take them through Abraham Maslow's "Four Stages of Learning". Before a coach brings someone's blind spot into the open to address, the coachee was *unconsciously incompetent*. They didn't know what they didn't know. Now the coachee is trying something new, and since they haven't mastered that yet, they will likely fail. Now they are *consciously incompetent*.

Failing at something new early and often is when it's easy to stop doing something and go back to the old ways. This time frame is when the commitment to care for the plan from the coach is critical. The checking-in, the following up, the accountability is what changes the game here. It raises the need for the person who is failing at their plan to push past incompetence and become *consciously competent*. This new competence is where the rubber meets the road on coaching, and you get to celebrate "coaching wins" together as you move toward the goal of the coachee becoming *unconsciously competent*. Things become muscle memory.

It's not uncommon for an employee going through coaching to fail, mess something up, and give up by going back to their old ways. Sometimes, they don't want to tell their coach because they may fear your reaction, especially if you're their manager and you have a tendency to react in a way they perceive as unfavorable. If you want your people to grow, it's best if you stop being a jerk! Seriously, you wouldn't be mean to a toddler who's learning to walk for falling over, would you? Other times they don't want to let their coach down, so they fear talking about it. Other times, they don't think a conversation about it can help, or maybe they don't believe the coach cares if they do it or not, so they don't bring it up. I don't recommend writing them off as "uncoachable" and giving up.

On the coach's side, to address all three of these reasons, they must completely let go of any agenda they have and be willing to

Chapter 4: Set Your GPS   77

look at a situation objectively. Asking questions such as these can get the coachee back on track:

- How is that working for you?
- Is doing that still important to you?
- When you don't (insert plan or commitment), what gets in the way?
- Have you tried it enough to determine if it works or not? How so?
- What is preventing you from bringing barriers like this up to me proactively?
- How will you do it better moving forward?
- What can I do to help you follow through with this moving forward?

Since coaching is a gift you give to others, it's up to them to decide what they will do with this gift. Now, if they choose to destroy your donation or chuck it in the trash time and time again, you've got to deal with it. Only you as the coach decide when they are crossing the line and not meeting your expectations. Let them know how you feel about it and the consequences if they continue doing that.

A great comparison to this is an issue I've recently addressed with my fifteen-year-old son Jack. My wife and I bought him a chrome book for school and a USB headset for gaming. Within the past month, Jack has dropped his chrome book, destroying the display. Then he left his USB headset on the ground, carelessly tripping over the cord while walking across the room texting, and ripping the connector off the wire. He's lucky enough to be tall and clumsy like his father. That being said, accidents and negligence are two different things.

I sat down with Jack and explained that his computer and headset are covered under warranty and that I would cover the replacement cost this time. I set the expectation that if negligence caused him to break his stuff again, he would be responsible for purchasing new ones out of his pocket. I'm not going to let my own son take the gifts I give him for granted. I also won't let a coachee take the time and energy investment it takes to help them grow with coaching and be negligent with that gift.

Here's my rule of thumb. If someone doesn't follow through, I'll coach them through their obstacles. No harm, no foul. As pointed out above, when coaching people, many issues and failures are expected, and they are a natural part of growth and not the exception to the rule.

Reoccurring issues that we've already coached through are a different story. As soon as I begin to see a pattern and begin to feel someone may have some of the traits I want to avoid coaching, I take action. I set the expectation like this, "For you to gain the most from our coaching relationship, I need to know you take your growth seriously. When you don't follow through with your commitment and plan after we coach, it makes me feel like you don't want to grow. If you continue to choose not to grow despite our coaching conversations, we will stop having them and instead I will coach someone who will value them. Would you like to continue to work together to grow through coaching?"

It's okay if they say no; the wrong person got past your red velvet rope. Let them out of the club and find the right person. You and someone who is "coachable" for you will both benefit. Think about it this way, let's say you have a team of twenty employees, and fifteen love your coaching and five don't. What if you doubled down on investing in the people that value it? What would happen if you gave 25% more coaching time and energy to the fifteen who use it? How would their careers and success be impacted? What would that mean for your team's results? As success increases for those you invest in, what happens to the five who don't accept your gift? You may find that the people who choose not to grow, the ones who don't value coaching, will likely fall behind. Like a computer that isn't upgraded, they will likely slow down and need to be replaced altogether.

My current checklist for determining if someone is "coachable" for me:

1. Did I coach them on what I want or what they want?
2. Did I help them realize the plan can get them what they want?
3. Did I support them in the way they asked?
4. Did something out of their control get in the way?
5. Did they have the ability to do that plan?
6. Is this a new issue that we haven't coached on before?
7. Did I openly discuss that my expectations aren't being met?

This process is a lot different from the 3-step program I outlined at the beginning of this section. This way, I know if I am fair to the person I am coaching or not.

If you're an employee reading this and you want to avoid being deemed uncoachable, you may want to consider the following:

1. Did I listen to understand my manager or coach, or was I on the defensive?
2. What if the manager giving me coaching wants the best for me?
3. When I committed to the plan, did I not take it seriously?
4. Am I behaving irresponsibly or unprofessionally?
5. Am I disrespecting my leadership and not respecting their time and the time of others that could benefit?
6. Am I open to personal growth or fighting change?
7. How can I grow if I know everything?
8. If I were a manager and an employee behaved like me, would I be okay with that?

Remember, coaching is a two-way street, and it's the ultimate form of leadership. In my opinion, the most effective way a leader can communicate with each person on their team is by coaching. Coaching is also the most effective way that someone who wants to grow can achieve what they want. Look at it in that way—leaders seek to give that gift always, and employees accept it with open arms. Watch what new heights you can achieve together.

Goals

Traveling across the country, you would want to decide what landmarks you want to visit, where you would need to refuel, and at what restaurants to eat. Some of these goals would be fulfilling to achieve; others are simply required to get where you want to go. As it relates to an employee's success, goals are simply the employee's

Chapter 4: Set Your GPS

personal benchmarks that they want or need to achieve on the way to their vision for success. You will need to work with them to develop and clarify short-term goals, mid-range goals, and long-term goals.

Most people think of a goal as something measurable like an income amount, sales volume increase, project time frame completion, losing X amount of weight, buying a new house or car, etc., and that is something you can list! The important thing to understand is what else a goal could possibly be! A goal may also be a feeling such as: satisfaction, success, peace of mind, stress/worry free, motivated, more optimistic, realistic, happier, attitude change, etc. A goal can also be a skill someone wishes to master: time management, leadership ability, selling and closing skills, organizational, communication, customer relations, project management, delegation, coaching skills, health & fitness, etc. Make sure to let your coachee know that goals come in all different types!

I remember working with one of my first official coaching clients back when I was charging 75 bucks an hour. Almost all the goals we set at the time seemed so distant. They were like looking at a distant building on the horizon. He wanted to start at the ground level and learn all that he could. He wanted to work in all aspects of the business (product/sales/customer service). He wanted to build lasting relationships with coworkers and clients. He wanted to increase sales. He also wanted to lead a team. It was an ambitious list! Yet, these were just his "short-term" goals. His long-term vision was to become COO of his company.

Well, we set all those "short-term" goals, and to my surprise he achieved every single one of them within the next six months. That left me scratching my head and thinking, "Well, what next?" I looked back at Jeremy's GPS. He had the vision for success and a purpose. That was what drove him.

That's when I learned two incredibly important lessons as a coach. First, when someone has a coach, they achieve their goals so much faster. Second, you never run out of things to coach on. After all, there are always more goals to be set until a person reaches that long-term vision for success. Even then, there's still places to go after that! That is, of course, as long as you coach them to help clarify their new vision for success!

Find Out What They Want

The first element to effective coaching is understanding what the people you coach want most. I believe a leader's job is to find out what each person on their team wants most and to help them achieve it. Every day someone works for you is a day they choose to follow you, and for that a true leader is grateful. Show your gratitude by helping those who work for you move toward what they want most in their lives and career. This activity creates superhuman loyalty to the leader. Reality is that employees are more likely to work for and help a leader succeed when they know that leader cares about them. What better way to show employees you care about them than to seek out and possess a deep understanding of their vision for success and help them make it a reality?

Imagine if you will that you are a merchant in a developing country and the only way for you to get your merchandise to the market for sale is by getting your donkey to lug it across town. Your donkey won't move! You try pushing the donkey, and it won't budge. In fact, it tries to kick you! You try grabbing its reigns and pulling the donkey, and it just yells at you with that crazy "Hee-haw" sound donkeys make. So, what do you do? You grab an apple, wave it in front of your donkey, and the next thing you know he's following you because you have what he wants. You've now caused movement and with much less effort than trying to push or pull the immovable object that is the donkey. What each employee truly wants is their apple. They're willing to help you get what you want only when they see that they can get what they want along the way. Remember the bunny in the room with the X and the carrot? Same thing.

Here are some questions I ask when trying to get to know someone and figure out what it is that they want.

- What is your ideal career?
- If everything worked out perfectly in a perfect world, what would work be like?
- How would you interact with others?
- How many people would answer to you?
- What skills would you have mastered?
- What would you be most respected for?
- What key values have helped you get to this ideal end state?
- What behaviors have become part of your routine to get to where you are in this career utopia?
- What is your day-to-day routine like in this vision of success?

So, what new possibilities are created when a manager seeks clarity around an employee's personal vision for success? How can knowing what each person wants help eliminate or mitigate turnover? How does it drive motivation?

Let's say the manager stops pushing their employee to do what they want and begins to focus on learning what the employee wants most.

Scenario one, the employee's vision for success is aligned to the company's. This sounds like an easy one to handle, but this can often stump managers when what an employee wants doesn't seem possible to help them achieve or isn't possible right now. The employee wants career growth, which can certainly help the company grow. So, what's the problem? Case in point: Career Development is one of the ten employee motivation requirements. How many times do people want to move up in their organization but there isn't a manager "spot" open?

I remember as a very young manager dealing with this conundrum with selfish thoughts of scarcity, "I can't teach them how to take my job, and there isn't a job for them available. If I teach them how to be a manager, they might leave and go be one somewhere else." If you're thinking this way now or have thought this way in the past, don't feel bad. Self-preservation is a natural human instinct. Now, let me show you a better way by asking you a few coaching questions.

- What expectations or results would it take for this employee to earn the right to receive mentoring and career development coaching from you?

- What would need to occur for you to move up in your organization and free a spot for them to move up?
- How would it be possible for you to work together with this employee so everyone wins?

Here the manager has two choices. They can either develop the employees to help them move toward their goal or avoid/diminish/ignore/marginalize their desire to move up. Compare the two scenarios. If you don't develop them, how long will they last within your organization without belief there is an opportunity to move up? If you do develop them, how long will they stick around your organization? Which scenario creates more loyalty, reciprocity, results, and positive impact? Which increases the likelihood of a long-term relationship and more success for everyone involved?

To slightly modify a Richard Branson quote: "*Coach* people well enough so they can leave, treat them well enough so they don't want to."

Employees all over America feel they have hit a ceiling with their current employer. Once this feeling has set in, unless turned around, these employees often find themselves in search of a new job where they may move up in their career. As a result, human resource people or managers find themselves looking for a new employee to replace the skilled professional that left. Whether the ceiling they feel they've hit is perceived or real, this poses a challenge for employers who depend on tenure and experience as a building block to company success.

As a manager, the question becomes, "Why don't you do something to prevent this tenured employee who wants to grow from leaving?" Most employers reply, "We simply can't promote everyone!" They use this as an excuse to live with the problem.

Instead of living with this problem, knowing full well we can't promote everyone, let's talk about 5 ways to solve this challenge. The key objective being to give your employees the feeling that they are moving up regardless of their duration in their current job role. In doing this, you will help your team improve and stay engaged, even if they are locked in their current role for the time being.

Uncover Their Strengths

Question what strengths your employees are not utilizing in their current role. This will shed light on what potential responsibilities you could give a particular employee to help them feel they are growing in their career. Allowing them to start unlocking their strengths to help impact your organization positively will help meet this crucial growth need.

Create Opportunity

After discovering which employees feel they are not moving upward, you can further discover ways you could better utilize their skills. Is there potential to give them more responsibility or more duties that would allow them to showcase their talents and also help your organization? Can you work out a win/win/win where the employee, the business, and the customer all benefit from the move?

Set Realistic Expectations

Set realistic expectations with them on what the new role entails. Often people want to move up but aren't capable of taking on a new role. The disconnect stems from blind spots or being unaware of exactly what the new role entails. Sitting down and reviewing what skills are necessary, what the expectations would be to move up, and what it takes to succeed in that next role are extremely important. Many times you can set them on the right path to reach their goal. Or they may decide moving up doesn't seem as appealing anymore. Either way, once they understand the real responsibilities that they will have to face down you will discover if you are grooming the right person for the next level in your organization. The key is the employee knowing they are moving toward their goal, even if the position is not available yet.

Measure Progress

Show them another way to measure career improvement by proving to them they are moving in the right direction! Again, since career improvement is not always measured by promotions or pay raises, we can capitalize with other means. What areas of development could you track to help the employee grow that could ultimately impact their pay, their skills, and the success of the company? The key being regular, ongoing aspiration coaching, proving to them regularly that they are moving forward by uncovering, acknowledging, and celebrating their wins. Another opportunity is often creating scorecards around their current job responsibilities, showing them what excellence looks like in each area, and helping them strive toward excellence.

Meet Other Needs

Ensure other employee motivation needs are met or exceeded! Have you ever heard an employee say, "You know, even though I don't get X or Y at my employer, I stay because of Z!" I'm not giving you a license to ignore the lack of development and career growth problem. I'm just pointing out that there are many other needs employees have to feel engaged. We will talk more about those in chapter 11. If you are able to meet those needs, you can keep employees engaged and essentially create an environment that is "good enough," which could prevent much of the unnecessary turnover.

These 5 key tactics can certainly help meet the employee career advancement need without actually promoting someone. This will help you lower turnover, increase tenure, create employees that will do what it takes to succeed, and make you a hero of a leader for your organization!

The best example I can share here was a coaching conversation between myself and a sales professional by the name of Tommy. In the era B.C. (before coaching), when employees would come to me wanting a promotion, I would usually handle it the same way every time. I would dismiss and procrastinate because I didn't believe they were cut out for the role or dismiss and procrastinate because there wasn't a spot open for them. My first year working with Tommy had been no different. Tommy was a seasoned automotive salesperson, just over 60 years of age, and he happened to be one of my top performers. At this time, he was selling 30ish units per month, which was great for a top producer in our market at our store. Tommy had come to me almost weekly to discuss his career development and I almost always brushed him off.

Despite his hard work and dedication to selling cars, there were a myriad of reasons I felt disqualified Tommy from being a manager. To name a few, Tommy didn't have much patience with customers who took some outside the box thinking and doing to come to an agreement. People throughout the dealership felt like Tommy could be a little brash when dealing with customers and other employees at the dealership. Some people, including myself, felt he had a pretty negative attitude. Tommy would help train some of the newer people, but some of them had a hard time using some of the word tracks he would teach them. In addition, Tommy would skip steps in our process if he felt like it would benefit him or his sales. With all the business he would create, I found that there was an equal amount of paperwork or customer satisfaction clean-up that had to be conducted, often by myself or the other managers when Tommy wasn't willing.

There were other expectations that Tommy wasn't meeting, so, of course, when he would come to me asking for a promotion, my gut reaction was to basically ignore him by pointing out something he didn't do right that was an area of frustration to me and then dismissing him. This led to a fifteen-minute argument roughly once a week where Tommy would explain why he should be a manager and I tried to explain what he needed to do right. That was the routine until the A.C. era of my leadership revolution when I started actually coaching. Once I did, I was a new form of leader who had adopted and was seeking to master the language of coaching.

As such, I was ready to coach Tommy on this subject. Engaging him was no longer a nuisance; it was my responsibility to help him achieve what he wanted in his career, regardless of how many hurdles we would need to overcome together. I realized every day he made a choice to work for me, and I owed it to him to give him the coaching he needed to move up in his career if he wanted. And if he was willing to put forth the effort it would take to be a leader in our business, then I would be willing to put in the effort to help him get there. This is when I realized the power of aspirational coaching, helping each person on your team achieve their aspirations by giving them the time, attention, tools, and support they need.

Excited about the opportunity to add value to my loyal employee, I proactively sought him out. "Tommy, it would be my honor to see you move up in your career. Would you like to sit down this evening, or tomorrow morning to discuss how you can achieve that?"

Tommy seemed to feed off the energy and blurted out, "This evening!"

Upon sitting down with Tommy, I recruited him to my conversation. "Tommy, I want for you to be able to reach the level in your career that you are most satisfied with. If you want to achieve career growth, I believe it's my responsibility to help you achieve it. Are you ready to discuss what that would look like?"

"You know I am, Boss," Tommy replied.

"First off, what does a manager in our business need to be good at?" I questioned with the goal of uncovering where he would need to grow as a leader before earning the promotion.

"Recruiting employees, closing deals, and training," he replied.

"What makes you say those three things?" I asked while I lined through those three management responsibilities on my sales management routine checklist.

"Well, because we need to find employees to replace the ones that don't make it. We have to save deals for our employees. And I do training for new people all the time, and that's really important."

I had recently built out my entire routine for coaching on time management, and his description was far too vague for my liking. I had to get more information, "And what sort of things are managers responsible for here?"

"Well, obviously selling cars, and hiring employees, and buying cars. Also, making sure the department is profitable," he stated.

"What else Tommy?" I asked.

"Hmm, giving sales meetings and dealing with angry customers… Oh, and I know our online reputation is really important nowadays," he added.

I could tell he was running out of stuff to add. "Anything else?" I wanted to make sure he emptied his bucket.

He thought about his answer a bit longer and replied, "Oh, the goal setting you do and keeping the sales board up to date." There was a pause while he was thinking, "I think that's about it."

Looking down at my list of routine items, I had lined through the ones Tommy had pointed out and noticed the other 75 responsibilities still unnamed on the list. Clearly, I had to do a better job communicating what my managers' jobs entailed to the sales team.

Even though there was a great opportunity to address his missing puzzle pieces for the management responsibilities and skills, I wanted to get his job role expectations and responsibilities out in the open. In addition, I wanted to see how Tommy viewed his strengths, so I asked, "What expectations are you doing a good job of meeting that would make me want to promote you and help you qualify for the role?"

Tommy was great at pointing out what was great about him and clearly wanted to sell himself as a manager to me, "Well, I sell a TON of cars, so I make more profit than anyone at the dealership. I'm the only one that comes in and works Sundays when we're closed. I'll work even harder as a manager and expect everyone else to do the same."

"I have no doubt about your work ethic and ability to sell," I agreed. "And you're really consistent with using the CRM and shooting videos to our internet shoppers. I appreciate your easy adoption and adaptation to using the technology we invest in."

"You're welcome, Boss! I didn't know you noticed!" He appreciated the validation and recognition, which is also one of the ten employee motivators, outlined in chapter 11, I might add.

I probed for the other half of the equation, "Now, what expectations are you not meeting that you'll need to meet in order to earn a promotion?"

Tommy said, "I probably need to do a better job of getting my paperwork done right."

"What else could get in your way?" I asked, knowing he was missing a lot of missed expectations.

"Well, I don't necessarily think it's my expectations that are holding me back. I sell far too many cars to get promoted. That's why I've been stuck as a salesperson most of my life. I sell too many cars. Top salespeople don't get promoted in the car business," he shared candidly.

This was not the case, and I had to coach him around this limiting belief right away. "A year and a half ago when I started, who were the top salespeople?"

Tommy listed them out, "Jake, myself, I.T., Fred, Tony, and Scott."

"And since then how many of those have gotten a promotion?" I asked.

"Well, two of them, but one is related to the owner. I'm not that lucky!" he rebutted.

"Okay, I want for you to know exactly what it's going to take for you to move up, and you have every right to know exactly where you'll need to grow. I am willing to share these things with you now, and to help you come up with a plan and work with you regularly to help you achieve your career goals. Are you ready to take some notes on this now?" I was ready to lay down the path he had never had clarity on and address his false beliefs.

"You bet," he braced himself to take notes, pen up, focusing on the legal pad in front of him.

"First off, so we're clear, I was the top salesperson at my dealership when I was promoted, and that was one of my fears, too. It wouldn't be fair if the top producing employees did not have a shot at career growth because they were penalized by their success. I want to point out that this in no way will hold you back. In fact, it is a requirement to move up that you're meeting. One requirement you have not yet met is the ability to duplicate yourself. I will expect that you help someone else, at least one other person, achieve better results before you earn a promotion." I paused a moment for that to sink in and then hit him with a question. "What results are the new hires you've been training generating from your time with them?"

He thought about it a moment and replied, "Not much, and they won't do what I teach them."

"Tommy, that's because we've given them the foundation of training on our sales process, and they've been tested for competency, and now they need coaching. The word tracks that work for you aren't the same ones that a twenty-something year old female can use. You'll need to learn to coach to be the most effective manager." I let him catch up on his note taking.

"Leading by example is critical to success, and one example I require of any leader is the ability to remain positive and professional at all times while following our process. This means respecting others in all situations, and keeping a positive attitude and remaining patient, even when things don't go well." I went on.

"Another misconception I want to address is what you said about recruitment. Finding bodies to throw at the sales floor is the opposite of what I want to accomplish. In fact, I want my managers to be experts at retaining employees more than finding new ones." I decided to pin the discussion on his expectations and switch gears to the management responsibilities because there was a large rift between what he knew and the reality of the responsibility, and I wanted to gain his input.

"How do you feel about meeting those first few expectations?" I asked.

"I'll need some training on those things, and I'll definitely have to change my ways, which will be tough, but I'm open to it," he replied.

"Okay, now let's go over the management responsibilities, and how they are measured by the owners of our company." I spent the next thirty minutes going over all the management responsibilities he hadn't mentioned from inventory stocking, merchandising, to reconditioning processes, then personnel responsibilities, reporting, and cross functioning department responsibilities.

By the end of the conversation I asked, "Now that you have clarity on what expectations you'll need to meet, and what you'll be responsible for as a manager, what questions or concerns do you have?"

Tommy looked at his notes with a frown on his face. Sounding slightly let down he replied, "Well looking at all this, I have made a decision. I don't want to be a manager anymore." Then he laughed out loud and said, "At least I can be a total jerk to you guys now!"

I half-heartedly smiled at his joke while grimacing to myself and thinking, "What have I done?" I asked him, "When you say don't want to be a manager anymore, what do you mean?"

As if reading my mind, Tommy said "Look, jokes aside, I need to do better on my paperwork, stick to the process more, and I know my attitude gets crappy sometimes. I'm going to work on that no matter what. That being said, you've made me realize that if I did become a manager, it would be even more stress than I have now. I would end up working even harder and, to be frank, it would have been a mistake because I don't want to do all that on your list. I'm grateful that you took time to go over this with me. I'll just keep selling, I suppose."

I was completely surprised at his change of heart, and seeing Tommy's mixed feelings of relief and dismay for letting this dream of being a manager go, I realized the huge mistake I had made in this coaching conversation. I wouldn't make this mistake again. I had never asked WHY this was important to him. I rectified that immediately. "Tommy, why is being a manager so important to you anyhow?"

He looked me square in the eye and shared something else I would have never expected his confident self to say in a million years. "You know, Sean, I'm in my sixties, I will be retiring in the next 5 or 6 years…" he paused while deciding whether getting vulnerable with me made sense or not. "If I retire as a salesperson, I will feel like a loser."

I was dumbfounded, another answer I would have never expected to hear, and that's how I learned to ask the why question at the onset of every coaching conversation. I thought about his answer and replied, "Tommy, you're probably in the top 1% of salespeople across the entire country. You've made an amazing career and life out of the car business and have achieved success selling that most people only dream of. I hope you can retire knowing you had one hell of a great career! You may retire being called a lot of things but 'loser' is not one of them."

He smiled gratefully.

Before he could say anything to me, I added, "And I'll tell you what, you give me 6 months' notice before you retire, and I'll make you an honorary manager. If you stick with me to that point, you will retire as a manager but won't have to do all the stuff that it takes to be one!"

When we got done laughing, he looked at me and asked, "You would do that for me?"

"Absolutely," I replied.

Tommy put his hand on my shoulder and said, "In all my years, no one's taken the time to sit down and go over things with me like this. Thank you, Boss."

Tommy never asked me for a promotion again, and his attitude, paperwork, ability to coach others consistently, and even his sales improved until I launched my business and left the company. In this conversation, I was able to address one of managers' greatest challenges, how to address employees who want a promotion when there isn't a spot for them right now. I also learned that one proactive hour-long conversation can save dozens of fifteen-minute blow ups, and a lot of other heartache.

Most leaders don't address challenges like this through coaching, and, as such, their people don't have a chance to decide if they want to grow or not. I learned that asking WHY for any coaching topic is critical to an effective co-created action plan. I learned that staying true to my values and goal to help other people achieve what they want most in their career was extremely energizing. On top of all that, this coaching conversation is a wonderful example of how asking great questions will undoubtedly get you great answers that will often surprise you.

Now, let's examine scenario two. The employee's vision isn't aligned to the team or company's direction. Here's where that "selling" manager in each of us, you know the part of us that fears a tenured employee quitting and wants to convince this valuable employee to stay with the company, often rears its ugly head!

I had just begun coaching one of the top Chrysler Dodge Jeep Stores in my state. I was working with one of the managers when a salesperson came in and began discussing his future. The salesperson brought up purchasing property and doing real estate in the future. The manager immediately began trying to talk the salesperson out of the future career change.

"You should stay focused on selling cars. You're already vested in this career, and you can make as much money as you want selling here." The manager sounded concerned and annoyed at the same time.

The salesperson immediately picked up on the manager's sales tactics. He knew the manager wasn't interested in helping his cause, or even understanding his point of view, and immediately went on the defensive.

"Look, I just thought with Sean here I could get some coaching on what I want to do. I'm sorry I even brought it up." The salesperson walked out of the office frustrated.

When I am working, situations like this present themselves all the time, and I call them coaching opportunities. To get buy-in from the manager around the coaching opportunity that presented itself, I recruited the manager to the conversation. "What I want for you is to have meaningful positive conversations with your employees where everyone, including you and the employee, wins. Is now a good time to discuss some ways you can do that?"

"Please!" The manager sounded grateful for the opportunity to receive some impactful coaching.

I replied with a question, seeking to understand how he felt that conversation went, "In your opinion, how did that conversation go?"

"Not very well," he replied candidly.

I asked, "What makes you say that?" I wanted to see if we were on the same page.

"I guess because I am frustrated, and he didn't seem too happy about it, either." He seemed a little unsure.

Not wanting to make the same mistake the manager made, I asked an open-ended question with no intent to sell the manager on something, "What were you trying to accomplish with the advice you gave your salesperson?"

He replied, "He's a good salesperson, and I think if he just keeps selling cars and focuses solely on that, he will be able to make the money he wants."

"In a perfect world, what else would you have accomplished in your dialogue with Steve?" I questioned deeper.

He thought about it for a moment and stated, "Also, it's hard to find good salespeople, and the last thing I need is him quitting on us."

My assumption was that he was trying to sell the salesperson on staying with the company, his answer certainly backed that up, but I wanted to verify the missing puzzle piece while also checking for his assumption. "What I am hearing is that your reply came from a desire to retain your awesome employee."

He nodded in agreement, "That is correct."

"Also, that you believed his reasoning for wanting to flip houses is financial because you mentioned he could make all the money he wants selling cars. Is that correct?"

"That is also correct," Adam said.

"Other than wanting to make more money, what else could he want to accomplish?" I questioned.

After some thought he replied, "Maybe he is bored with selling cars. Flipping houses might be a new adventure for him."

"Maybe he inherited a fixer upper and wants to unload it?" I joked but realized it could also be a possibility. "What do you really understand about his situation and the why or reasons behind what he brought up?" I probed.

"Not much." He laughed at himself

The manager realized he was making some costly assumptions. Coaching helped him uncover that he was assuming the worst-case scenario, out of fear of loss.

"How could the desire to invest in real estate positively affect his car sales?" I asked.

It didn't take long for the light bulb to blink on, "He would literally have to sell more cars in order to afford to invest in real estate!"

As a result of this coaching conversation, I was able to give the sales manager coaching tools, and facilitate a conversation between the manager and salesperson that allowed an effective one-on-one to take place. The manager stopped trying to sell the employee on "selling cars" and as such the following discussion and action plan unfolded.

The salesperson was open with the manager and the fact that he wanted to see if he could move out of his neighborhood while rehabbing and flipping his current house. In reality, the salesperson had no intention of quitting the dealership anytime soon. The coaching questions the manager asked helped the salesperson uncover that he would need a fair amount of liquid capital to afford rehabs. As such, we coached and came up with a game plan to increase his sales by 5 cars per month to fund his rehabbing. In this case, we aligned effort with goals and everyone won. The alignment for mutual success was there, and everyone came out ahead. The manager didn't need to worry about losing an employee to another industry, and the employee not only created a plan to sell more which made a positive impact on the business, but the employee also learned the value the manager placed in him at their dealership. None of this would have been possible without effective coaching.

Chapter 5

The First Type of Coaching: Aspirational Coaching

In previous chapters, you have gotten your mind right for coaching while getting ready to stretch your comfort zone, braced yourself for growth, and realized the need to learn to communicate even more effectively with coaching. Then we helped you identify what coaching is, and what coaching isn't. We have laid the foundation for successful coaching by giving you your new tool to understand what truly motivates each person you get to coach in the G.P.S. Now, it's time to give you the processes to turn these concepts into reality, and the structure necessary so that you'll be able to tactically execute effective impactful coaching.

After conducting thousands of paid coaching conversations on every subject imaginable as it relates to career and business for everyone from software company executives, dealership owners, sales professionals, middle managers, operations directors, non-profit board members, service professionals, global trainers, religious leaders, conference organizers, political leaders and more, I have found that all of the coaching conversations I have had fit into one of these four categories:

1. Aspirational Coaching
2. Metric Coaching
3. Observational Coaching
4. Turn Around Coaching

Each type of coaching yields its own unique benefits as you will see from the examples throughout the next few chapters. Since the base foundation for all the coaching you will do is aspirational coaching, we will start by learning about that.

Aspirational coaching is investing scheduled time and focused energy into helping others accomplish their goals, career, and personal aspirations following a proven process for people development with measurable success.

For aspirational coaching, I want you to look at your employees like bank accounts, not literally but figuratively. You can't withdraw what you have not deposited. Conducting aspirational coaching is making massive deposits into the employee's account. The deposit in aspirational coaching is your investing your time and energy in helping them get what they want. In this way, you earn the right to make withdrawals when you ask them to help you get what you want. It's a beautiful thing in leadership when both of these things happen to align. Talk about a win-win!

Masterful coaching from a manager occurs when a leader becomes proficient at connecting the dots between the two: what the manager wants the employee to do and what the employee wants to gain from doing that. You will see this unfold in all its splendor in the coaching example I share in this chapter. There are several benefits of aspirational coaching:

- Create extreme motivation
- Deepen your relationships with employees
- Bind the team
- Enhance your brand as a leader

- Drastically decrease employee turnover.

For now, let me walk you step-by-step through the all-powerful D.R.I.V.E.C3™ Coaching Framework. After doing so, we will outline a real D.R.I.V.E.C3™ coaching conversation that will help you see each element of the framework in real time use. You will then understand how aspirational coaching achieves the benefits outlined above.

D - Discover What They Want in the Future and What They Want Now

This step requires selflessness, a desire to put others' desires and goals ahead of your own, and a desire for clarity. Perhaps you've heard the saying, "Nobody cares how much you know, until they know how much you care." Great news, you've already done the GPS so you know what they want in the future. Check! Just by asking and learning about what your employee wants to accomplish in the long term, they know you care. But what do they want to gain right now? For this tactical aspirational coaching conversation, you need to know. This is how a coach ensures each person on their team is on the right road, going the right direction. That's the point of the D in D.R.I.V.E.C3™. Discover how you can help them right now, and why that matters to them (the significance). Remember, you can't coach the HOW, until you know the WHAT and the WHY.

Five great questions to discover the "what" are:

- "What conversation needs to take place right now, in order for you to continue to move toward your vision for success?"
- "What would make today's conversation extremely valuable for you?"
- "If there were one outcome from today's coaching conversation that would give you confidence to know you were on the right path, and make your life/work exponentially easier, what would it be?"
- "Where in your business/life/career do you want coaching to impact your success today?"
- "For you to achieve what you want most, what should we focus our discussion on right now?"

The second half of the D in Discover = Significance. This is how you find out the WHY behind the what. In Simon Sinek's book *Start with Why* Simon talks about how the world would be forever changed if everyone started with WHY instead of with WHAT in their messaging and conversation. While we wait for that to happen, it's important to uncover the why with great questions. Here are four of my favorite questions that will help you uncover this and one coaching statement. (Yes, statements may be used in coaching!)

- "Of everything we could have coached on today, why is this so important for you?"
- "When we accomplish that in our conversation today, what will that mean for you?"
- "How will coaching on this help you achieve what you want most in your vision for success?"

- "Why is this a key coaching conversation for you right now?"
- "Help me understand the true significance of this conversation today."

It is important to note that in the discovery phase, you may come across two, three, or more areas to coach on. This is where the need to create clarity and alignment comes into focus. In most coaching situations, you won't have the time to coach on more than one or two areas of opportunity in one conversation. Sometimes, you have to point blank ask something like this, to create clarity, and know exactly where your focus should be. "Based on what you've said so far, there are three areas we could coach on right now. Which one of these topics is most important to discuss first?"

Remember, aspirational coaching is a gift for them. Even if one of those 3 topics is more fun for you to coach on, or you feel like the one they pick isn't as important, let them choose. It's their topic, their agenda. Then remember, that no problem can be solved without clarifying said problem. That's the whole point of the Discover step, just having the surface level goal or challenge probably isn't enough to coach them yet. Ask one or more of the following clarification questions:

- "What is getting in the way of your doing that now?"
- "If you were to list out all the barriers to accomplishing that right now, what would they be?"
- "When you've tried to solve this issue in the past, what obstacles did you run into?"

- "How has your progress been halted while moving in that direction so far?"
- "When that happens, what do you think is really going on?"

R - Recruit Them to Your Conversation

This step requires empathy and a desire to share your positive intent. You can't win a war with a one-person army. What you need to understand about communicating with others is that in the first fifteen seconds of any conversation, people choose one of two sides. Scenario one, they choose to fight against you, because they feel attacked. Maybe they feel your objective doesn't align with their goals, and as such the battle begins. If you're a manager, you know what I'm talking about. It might sound like this:

Executive: Why aren't you holding your people accountable?!

Manager: I can't hold them accountable when my hands are tied by HR policies and state laws!

Manager in his head thinks: *I knew I was on the hot seat ever since I missed those goals last quarter. I better start looking for a new job.*

The executive started with WHAT he wanted the manager to change. As such, the manager felt attacked, and immediately took up arms against the executive and deflected the assault to others. As a result of the lack of recruitment, the executive who is trying to create accountability had to fight against the manager. Not much good comes from conversations like this.

Chapter 5: The First Type of Coaching: Aspirational Coaching

How do you win a war? You build an Army! You need an army where multiple people are working together to win an objective or accomplish a mission. How do you build an Army? RECRUIT! I'm not referring to the traditional sense of hiring people here. What I am referring to is a recruitment statement where the coach wins the other party over to their cause and generates alignment to the conversation in the way they engage with the other party. With a positive recruitment statement, scenario two happens. Scenario two is that the other party realizes that you as the coach are joining their cause to help them achieve their objective. As such, the coach is able to create a collaborative effort, a force multiplier, where two brains are working together to achieve a common goal!

An effective recruitment statement might sound like this:

Executive: I want for you to know that each person on your team respects you as their leader. When could we sit down and discuss some ways to improve that even more for you?

Manager: That would be great, I'm open right now!

Manager in his head thinks: *I'm lucky to have a leader like this who always wants the best for me. I'm going to buy my boss and his wife a trip to the Bahamas.*

Okay, I may have exaggerated the last manager's thought, but you get the idea! When you begin your conversation with effective recruitment, you bring up what the other person can gain from the conversation first. You are giving them the gift of your positive intent. Note the "for you" twice throughout that conversation. Then you ask permission second. This removes the natural fear and anxiety that results from the other person's natural human instinct to believe the worst-case scenario.

Note the different reaction from the coachee. You see that through the recruitment methodology, the defensive posture from the manager is gone, and they are open to the discussion. Now we have two brains working together instead of two brains battling each other.

Recruitment isn't natural. Because it's our natural human tendency to focus on what we want, instead of what the person we are coaching wants. Here's how to break the habit, go against the grain, and engage others like a masterful coach instead of a typical frustrated manager.

How to create effective recruitment statements… It starts with the other person's desired outcome first! Along with my coach, Keith Rosen, I have developed my own strategy for consistently being able to recruit people to every conversation on a dime, second nature. It involves asking myself a few coaching questions just before engaging in the conversation. Here they are:

- "What does this person have to gain by making this change?"
- "How does making this change help this person accomplish what they want most?"

If I have good, tangible answers to those two questions, I know what I can recruit around. It's the answers to those questions! The next step is to insert "I want for you" into the beginning of the statement. This is what makes the conversation a gift for the coachee.

This is what shifts the dialogue from a manager pushing their agenda to a dialogue geared at helping the other person get what they want out of their career and life. Then add, "When is a good time to discuss this?" to respect the time of the person you want to coach and honor their schedule.

If the questions in the above strategy aren't working to help you form your recruitment statement, consider using this approach instead. Take the worst-case scenario outcome, or the negative result being created from the undesired behavior, and turn it on its head by asking yourself the following question:

> What is the exact opposite of the worst-case scenario, and the best possible outcome that could occur if they change?

The answer to this question will give you the meat of your recruitment statement. Now just sandwich it in between, "I want for you" and "When is a good time to discuss this?" Here's an example! Let's say you're wanting a salesperson to send personalized videos to prospects through their CRM but they refuse. By not sending videos, they're not getting as much engagement as they could from customers, it's costing them sales, they could miss their goals, and they won't be able to spend as much on their upcoming vacation! The exact opposite of those things would be: They will have more money to spend on their upcoming vacation by exceeding their goals when selling as much as possible by getting more engagement from their prospects!

I want for you to + have more money to spend on your upcoming vacation by exceeding your goals when selling as much as possible by getting more engagement from your prospects! + When is a good time to discuss some ways to make this happen? = Recruitment Statement

As it relates to recruitment, the greatest mistake leaders make in their conversations is when they start by telling people what they need to do, or how they need to do it instead of beginning with what the other person can gain from having this conversation about change in the first place. Recruit to get the buy-in, and you get to multiply the brain power. When you recruit and there are two brains working together to achieve more, you end up with the equivalent of four brains. When you fail to recruit, one brain is battling another, and they kill each other off. You end up with no brains. Most importantly, the approach from the senior leader always affects the mindset and triggers something in the person being approached. The question is, what do you want to trigger? Fear, anxiety, and stress or alignment, gratitude, and curiosity? Build or destroy. Grow or kill. Create scarcity or abundance. As the leader, you always get to pick, you're always in control of this, and it's all in your approach.

I -Inquire to Build the Puzzle

This step requires patience, curiosity, and actual listening. When it comes to your people's vision for success and goals, I want you to look at them accomplishing these things like solving a 1000 piece

Chapter 5: The First Type of Coaching: Aspirational Coaching

puzzle. I believe that when it comes to helping your people accomplish what they want to accomplish, they often have 95% of the puzzle pieces it takes in place. Within the 5% lies the coaching opportunity, where you as their coach get to help them finish the puzzle and achieve what they want.

Within the 5%, imagine 3% of the puzzle pieces are missing all together. Those puzzle pieces are "knowledge gaps," and this is where they need education and/or training. Then for the other 2% of the puzzle, they have the wrong pieces jammed into the wrong holes. They almost fit, but overall mess up the aesthetic of the puzzle and prevent them from solving it all the way. Look at these as limiting beliefs that are holding their success back. Your job as the coach is to ask enough questions to find out what 95% of the puzzle pieces they already have in place. You don't want to waste your valuable time and their precious energy by giving them puzzle pieces they already have. This is one of the fastest ways to diminish the value of your coaching.

Example: At the time of writing this book my five-year-old daughter Emma is a big art aficionado. You can tell by her Crayola crayon and marker art gallery covering my refrigerator. The other night she was using the giant painted whiteboard wall in my home office. I have a healthy selection of marker colors in the office up on a small shelf, purposefully out of her reach. (She has a tendency to smash the tips into the marker, but that's neither here nor there.) I had been accumulating enough, and she was bored while I was finishing up some Inspired Satisfaction cultural assessment summary documents. When Emma started coloring, she grabbed the black and red markers I had left sitting on my assistant's desk. Emma said to me, "Daddy, I need more colors!"

I looked down and noticed which two colors she already had. Being one of those parents who gets slight enjoyment from annoying his kids, I handed her a black marker.

"No, Daddy! I already have that one," she exclaimed with a cute look on her face, that revealed that she half suspected I did that on purpose, and half wondered if I wasn't paying attention.

"Oh! My apologies little one." I grinned as I handed her a red marker, identical to the one she had already gotten bored of coloring with.

"Daddy, I already have that one, too! I need a different one!" She complained with a giggle. "I can't make my picture better without more colors. Please help me!"

I thought about her plea, and how it related to coaching.

The lesson here is that when you give your kid markers they already have, it's funny. Also, when you give your employees puzzle pieces they already have, you're not helping them. Since they already do so many things right, if you just spew forth solutions, based on assumptions, without getting all the puzzle pieces out on the table, your odds of giving them a puzzle piece they don't have is like the odds of hitting a bullseye with a dart while blindfolded. Thus, you will need to ask a series of questions first. This may sound a lot easier than it actually is, and one of the most common coaching conversations I have with managers learning to coach their people is when they ask me, "How can I ask enough questions or more of the right questions?" In this section, I will give you tools to help you do just that.

Chapter 5: The First Type of Coaching: Aspirational Coaching

Thinking back to my pre-coaching telling, selling, and yelling manager days, there were so many circumstances where my employees needed some information and I was all too happy to provide it, way too fast. My employees liked me enough, or perhaps were annoyed enough, to tell me when I was giving them puzzle pieces they already had. Here are a couple signs that you may be guilty of doing this:

1. People straight up call you presumptuous, or assumptive.
2. You become frustrated with your employees when you tell them what to say, and they tell you, "I did that already." And "Tried that." Or "Been there, done that, Boss."
3. You frequently "win" arguments with your employees.

Okay, enough brow beating for doing it wrong; let's talk about how to do it right! In order to consistently grow as a business leader and coach, I read a lot of books and have invested a lot in my own personal development. At any given time, I am enrolled in at least one business course and have a minimum of two coaches. Not long ago, I took a Six Sigma course on what's called "root cause analysis". Six Sigma is strategy for improving efficiency in manufacturing, and I find it valuable because it helps managers zero in on issues that are six standard deviations out of the norm. It then helps them address the issues in the most efficient way possible. From this course, I learned what they call the "Five Why's". Essentially, they say the root cause of most issues is uncovered when you go five why's deep. In fact, I was able to use this in two conversations this week. One was with an executive who owns three car dealerships, and one was with a sales manager of a dealership. Here are the examples of how each of those worked.

Manager's Problem: My employees don't ask for referrals.
Why don't they ask for referrals?
They don't want to.
Why don't they want to?
They don't see value in it without immediate gratification.
Why don't they see immediate gratification?
They don't get the results because they don't do it right.
Why don't they do it right?
Root Cause: Because we don't train them and hold them accountable to doing it.
Solution: Train and roleplay with each employee. Require each employee to use the referral app during each customer delivery, and when they don't the deal will go up for grabs into a lottery for another salesperson to win later in the month.

Dealership Owner's Problem: When it snows, my employees just complain, don't want to work, and just want to go home.
Why do they complain?
They're used to business being handed to them on a silver platter.
Why are they used to getting business handed to them?
Because even if it's slow for a couple days, it picks up again.
Why does it get slow for a couple days?
Because they don't consistently prospect.
Why don't they consistently prospect?

Root Cause: Because of a bad habit loop. Employees complain and whine about it being slow because it makes them feel better since misery loves company. Complaining is easier than getting to work prospecting!

Solution: On a snow day, make work fun. BBQ for everyone and then create an appointment setting contest and pay them for setting 3 appointments like they sold a car. Stop tolerating whining and group complaining!

You see in both of these examples we got to the root cause. The root cause is where the rubber meets the road on empowerment and driving behavioral change. The tip of the iceberg didn't sink the Titanic; it was the enormous block of ice under the surface.

While the five why's are powerful for determining root cause, it still doesn't get you ALL the puzzle pieces. Before you can give them any value, you'll need to learn much more about their unique situation. You need to seek truth! These are the following items you'll need to explore further:

- What have they tried to address that issue?
- How did they conduct those activities?
- When did they try it?
- Who was involved?
- What results did attempting it that way yield?
- How did the other party/parties react?
- What has changed since then?
- What did they think about trying but haven't yet?
- What stopped them from trying that?

Framing coaching conversation specific questions around each of these key areas will help you uncover the truths. By uncovering the truth, you have earned the right to add value. The best part is, when it comes time to give them education, the questions you ask to help them create a solution will be that much more on point. You never have to worry about asking the wrong questions when you've asked enough questions to know their picture of reality: who, what, where, when, how, and why.

Active Listening VS Actual Listening

The last part of Inquiry I will point out to really help you hone your skills and be the best possible coach you can be for each person on your team is to define actual listening. Everyone talks about "active listening" where you're supposed to make eye contact, nod your head, and acknowledge their points. Active listening doesn't mean someone is *actually listening*. In fact, some people are so good at active listening, they can fool the other party into believing they were listening the entire time. Or worse, the other party can tell you're not really listening but for fear of embarrassment doesn't call you on it because accusation is never a pleasant experience for either party. For those of you who are married and reading this book, you probably know exactly what I am talking about! But our spouses don't often fear calling us on not listening, especially when we're pretending to do so. Bottom line is actual listening is something you do with your eyes, your ears, your head, your heart, and your soul. "WHOA!" You may be thinking! I know, that sounds deep, but let me explain.

You **listen with your eyes** when you are observant of the other person's posture, body language, and facial expressions. You are observing while they speak to ensure you take note of any misalignments between their words and their expressions. In addition, you are aware of your physical reactions and ensuring they see exactly how you feel. Be ready to explain your reaction in an honest manner. You're watching them react to thing things you say, and when that reaction seems concerning, defensive, or you're just not sure, you ask them to explain.

Example: "I noticed you turned away when I asked if your father wants you to take over the family business. Where did that reaction come from?"

You **listen with your ears** for tonality, stress, joy, fear, enthusiasm, and frustration, all the while seeking clarity. When you hear one of these emotions behind a word or sentence, and some additional context would help you further understand their point of view, open that can of worms.

Example: "When you said teamwork, you sounded excited. What about that gets you most enthusiastic?"

You **listen with your head** for facts, details, or lack thereof. You listen for contradictions, limiting beliefs, and assumptions. You curiously seek out more details even when you think you've gotten them all. You must try to avoid thinking of what question you're going to ask next, or what you're going to say, while they are speaking. As soon as you begin to do this, you've stopped listening with your mind. When you're listening with your mind, it's important to take shorthand notes. This will allow you to stay focused on their dialogue and loop back around to an important question or statement you need to make when the time comes.

Also, pause to think about their perspective and formulate a response before you say something. There is nothing wrong with a little silence in a conversation. Understanding this is key to effective coaching. When you reply without thought, you are giving away one of the only three things you have control over, your reactions. Even if you wrote down three shorthand questions to ask and one statement, there will be time to ask them once it's time. Also, when you ask questions from the brain, you are being objective. Avoid those "Selling" questions we talked about earlier in the book. Here your questions are objective with no agenda or expectation of a right answer. You're only seeking truth.

Example: "Earlier you said they never listen to you, and then you mentioned that your team has been working on something you tasked them to do. Can you give me clarity? Under what circumstances do they not listen to you?"

When you **listen from your heart**, you add empathy and love to your coaching. You must want with all your heart to help them achieve their goals; you must understand their point of view so you can feel their frustration toward their barriers, desire to achieve their goals, and excitement around their opportunity. Your heart is where your passion in helping them comes from and is also from where your best "Recruitment Statements" emerge. In addition, when you check for understanding by paraphrasing what they said, use empathy to reiterate how that might have felt to you.

Example: "I want for you to enjoy selling again so you can really knock the last few years before retirement out of the park. I can imagine if a change like that was made during my last few years at the dealership, I would feel pretty bummed out, too."

Listening with your soul requires faith. Luke 1:37 - *Faith doesn't make things easy; it makes them possible.* When you're actually listening, you trust in the person speaking with you. You believe that you can help them achieve what they want with your coaching and leadership. You have faith that they can and will succeed. You believe with every fiber of your being that they are ready and willing to face hard truths. The hard truths that you as their coach must shed light on which it takes to ensure they break free from the shackles of fear, low self-worth, apathy, resentment, and self-sabotage that's holding them back from fulfilling their God given potential. Listening with your soul isn't easy, but it will make their growth possible.

Let them empty the bucket!

As it relates to the inquiry stage in D.R.I.V.E.C3™: people will trust your advice when they know you understand their unique situation. Let me say that another way—people won't put value in your advice unless they feel like you've listened to them first and understand what the heck they are talking about. If the Discovery were the foundation for coaching, then the Inquiry portion is the structure that the rest of the conversation bolts onto. This step is absolutely critical to effective coaching and is one of the most difficult things to get right in coaching.

V - Verify You've Found their Missing Puzzle Piece and that it's Time to Add Value

The value trap. If you're anything like me, and chances are if you're reading this book you are, then you relish adding value. By "adding value," I mean giving someone something they don't have but know they need. As it relates to coaching, that means you may delight in giving someone the knowledge that will help them achieve what they want. That means seeing them adopt a new process you share that could change the game for them gets you excited. That means helping them adopt a new mindset that will help them overcome their greatest challenge makes you feel fulfilled. Personally, I love making that kind of impact for someone. How about you? There is a potential pitfall here, though. This mental payday can cause us to jump at the opportunity to add value, go down a rabbit hole with a dead end, and lose momentum while detracting from the value you can provide. This is the reason I added this step to the structure of D.R.I.V.E.C3™. If you feel the same way about those things as me, then you may end up in "the value trap". The value trap is when we jump into training, teaching, or educating before it's time to do so.

There are other reasons you may get stuck in the value trap. Maybe for you it's more about getting through the conversation and onto the next task. If that's you, then as soon as you hear what you believe is a knowing problem, you may have the tendency to start teaching and preaching. Again, you go down a rabbit hole with a dead end and lose momentum while detracting from the value you can provide. In rare circumstances, when I am in a "rushed" coaching conversation, I've sometimes taken the short cut of skipping this step. Often when I have, it ends up prolonging the conversation as I spend time reverting back to the Inquire phase after wasting valuable time and energy educating on something they didn't need. Whatever your reason, you want to avoid at all costs moving onto the next step without this verification. Here's an easy-to-understand example of what I'm talking about.

"I am so hungry!" says person one, looking at their watch wondering how long until it's time to eat.

"Don't worry, I got you covered, wait right there!" Person two jumps in the car, drives to McDonalds, waits in line for fifteen minutes, spends ten dollars on a double quarter pounder meal, and drives back to meet person one.

Person one waits out of respect for person two, constantly checking their watch wondering what's going on with person two.

Person two pulls in, rushes the food over to person one and says, "Here's food!" They're excited to provide value… in the form of artery clogging, sesame covered bun goodness.

"Uh, thanks but its Ramadan. I can't eat until sundown," person one says.

The eager burger delivery person had good intent, but, in reality, spent time, money, and energy on something that was irrelevant. They wasted their time and the time of the party they were "trying" to help. #CoachingFail

So where does the V come in? Verify the missing puzzle piece, with a question or two, or three.

Let's rewind and add this to the conversational example above!

"I am so hungry!" says person one, looking at their watch wondering how long until it's time to eat.

"What type of food are you hungry for?" asks person two, furiously seeking an opportunity to add value.

"I'd eat just about anything right now!" says person one.

"What's getting in the way of you getting something to eat?" questions person two.

"It's Ramadan, so I can't eat until dark," says person one.

Person two sought to verify the missing puzzle piece before trying to find a way to add value and uncovered that there wasn't one. The person did not need assistance around this particular scenario. This happens in coaching all the time. The coachee tells a story that we think is alluding to the area of opportunity where we can help, but that's not what they need. Make sure you ask enough questions to verify the missing puzzle piece, before adding value.

Ensure they empty the bucket, giving you ALL their puzzle pieces. Now you know what they know, what they don't know, what they have tried, and haven't. Thus, you're in the know and you know how to coach the know-it-all!

E - Educate – Bring Out from Within (Ex Duco)

It's the moment you've been waiting for. It's time to add value with education. Yet perhaps not in the sense you may be thinking. When you think about the word "educate" and picture that happening in your mind's eye, what do you see? You may see a teacher, standing in front of a class, pointing at something on a chalk board while telling the class something they need to know. Yet, this type of teaching is telling and training, not educating. To understand the reason I chose the word "educate" for my coaching process is to understand the root meaning of the word.

Educate comes from two Roman words, "e," meaning "out of" and "duco," meaning "to lead". So, education is when we are able to help the person we are educating, our coachee, by coaching the answers out of their heart and mind. We do this with, can you guess it? I'll bet you did, questions! With questions, people can arrive at their own answers and, when they do, they believe them.

This is the most powerful way of teaching, because when people say it, they believe it, and when they believe it, they remember it. You may have heard what they say about curriculum in school, that we only retain 10% of it, if that. This changes when you are posed a question and you create the answer. You will retain a much greater percentage of data when your mind works through the answer and arrives at its own conclusion. This is why the best way to educate is to ask instead of tell.

Another great benefit to asking, and helping them bring forth the answers from within, is that you get to find out where the limiting beliefs are. It's extremely important to point out that sometimes the answers that our coachee may arrive at are NOT in fact good answers. In fact, the answers that our coachee arrives at may hold back their success. My first coach and dear friend, Keith Rosen, calls limiting beliefs S.C.A.M.s, which stands for Stories, Cons, Assumptions, and Mindsets. Below there is an entire chapter about how to coach around limiting beliefs. But when a limiting belief comes up, like a weed in a garden, it's important that it is ripped out and destroyed at the root.

I was coaching with a high performing General Sales Manager of the fastest growing and one of the most successful Mercedes-Benz dealerships in the country, Sam Cavett. (Whom I want to congratulate for his recent promotion to General Manager.) Anyhow, Sam is not only a coaching client, but also a friend, and someone I look up to regarding faith because of his deep study of the Bible. We were talking about how limiting beliefs were like weeds, that they pop up, and sometimes salespeople will water each other's weeds, causing the roots to grow deeper. Water the weeds long enough and when they ripen, they'll sprout seeds and spread their chaos even further, destroying the once healthy garden by choking out all that was good. When I pointed this out to this faith-filled leader, he immediately quoted the Bible:

"'And I looked upon a stone wall, thorns and brambles and growth through it and it was in disarray. I took note.'" (Proverbs 24:31)

What took me a few minutes to realize was that Sam had connected the dots to what we were talking about and a powerful verse in the Bible. The verse was telling us that in building knowledge, order, and success, evil seeds of doubt, deceit, division, diversion, and dissent, if left unchecked, will destroy what has been built. It is the natural state of the world to devolve into chaos. By eliminating limiting beliefs and ridding the mind of these treacherous thoughts, you are helping to create order.

As a coach, it's your responsibility and deepest obligation to coach around these limiting beliefs, effectively ripping them out of the garden before they can consume it. Your job is to replace the story of those you're coaching with a better one that will give them the right attitude, actions, or reactions, which will help them achieve the desired results,. This is effectively tearing the weeds out of the cracks in the wall before they can separate brick and mortar. As their coach, you are charged to show them that their con is a lie, preventing them from further self-deception. You are expected to help them see that their assumptions are simply one possibility in a sea of other possibilities so that they can find out the friendly, or sometimes unfriendly, truth. You, as this person's coach, must help them see the outcome of their unhealthy mindset so that they may steer the ship out of harm's way right now. This coaching will help them prevent their ship from crashing into the iceberg of inevitable failure.

Leveraging the Three Perspectives

When educating someone through coaching, it's important to leverage the three perspectives. Leveraging the three perspectives reinforces the fact that you care. Remember what we said earlier about that. No one cares how much you know, until they know how much you care. The three perspectives ensure that you as the coach have earned the right to add value. Remember what else we discussed earlier, no one will trust your advice until they believe you understand their unique situation. The three perspectives also ensure the other person is able to let go of emotional attachments to a potentially unfavorable outcome. This is important because it's hard for someone to make a clear decision when they are emotionally attached to an outcome.

The first perspective is first person point of view. It's looking through the lens of the coachee. This is when you find out how they feel about a situation. This is when you show empathy and concern. This also helps you understand their WHY. Understanding the WHY is how you understand their WIIFM (What's In It For Me). This is what you will use to re-recruit them before taking a swing at educating, and before coaching them around their limiting belief.

Example: I was coaching a young lady, let's call her Aubrey. She had been furloughed from her sales position during the Covid pandemic. Her employer had asked her to come back, but she didn't want to go back anymore, and she was thinking about quitting. This was because she wasn't asked to go back first. They chose another sales rep that hadn't been with the company as long. As a result, they moved forward in bringing back several other employees before her.

Leveraging first person perspective first, I asked Aubrey, "How did that make you feel?"

The second perspective is second person point of view. This is when you help the other person explore how others involved may have felt. This helps the person you are coaching explore some of the potential "WHY"s from the other party(ies) involved. Since you can't know for sure how the other party truly felt without asking them directly, it's important to list out, essentially taking inventory of the possibilities. It helps them empathize with the others, walk in their shoes.

Example: "If you were the manager, how would you feel about one of your employees wavering on wanting to come back to work?"

The third perspective is objectivity. It's helping the coachee to become the coach on the sideline, watching a team play the game. While coaching executives, entrepreneurs, middle managers, and front-line employees, I've found it extremely useful to help the person I am working with step outside their own head, and emotionally detach. This must be done only after helping them clarify and define how they felt. Then by helping them understand the second party perspective. Now they can detach and make a clearer, better decision. This is where the What's and the When's come in, which segue into the How's when we move into the next phase of D.R.I.V.E.C3™.

Example: "Aubrey, now that we've explored how you feel here and we've discussed how your manager may have felt, are you open to looking at this objectively for a moment? What decision will help you achieve what you want in your business? What decision is most aligned to your personal core values?"

A frequently asked question I get as it relates to the "education" portion is this: "What if I don't know enough to teach someone something?"

That, my friend, is the least of your worries! At least, when it relates to coaching. How can I say that? To this day, I haven't yet run into a situation where I couldn't add value with some education. If you follow my coaching processes within this book, neither will you. That's because a large portion of the time you're coaching, they will come up with their own strategy which will just require some collaboration from you to hone. The rest of the time, if you're not ready to educate, it's only because you haven't asked enough questions in order to find the missing puzzle piece that you, as an individual, can provide. You always have some knowledge they don't, and because people can't read the label while they're inside the bottle and you're on the outside looking in, you'll always be able to add value… after you've asked enough questions.

C – Co-Create the Action Plan and Commit to it

Think of the last conversation you had that didn't go so well. Maybe you left the chat frustrated or feeling drained. Perhaps you're a manager and you were trying to correct or improve one of your people. On the other hand, maybe you're an employee, and you had a conversation with a client or supervisor, and the discussion left you feeling anxious, but you can't quite put your finger on why. After analyzing thousands of ineffective conversations between managers and employees, and employees and their customers, I've discovered that one of the main reasons why conversations are frustrating for one or both parties is a lack of commitment.

Remember this: the enemy of commitment is ambiguity.

The most subtle way people skirt commitment is with ambiguity, and ambiguity is the opposite of clarity. I define clarity by knowing who does what by when. An uncommitted person will avoid taking responsibility for the next action item and avoid being the "who" themselves. Let's look at how salespeople do this subconsciously when asking for referrals.

"Here are some business cards, and if you know someone who needs a car, I'd appreciate it if you'd send them to me."

There are two "who's" responsible for taking action in this example, and neither one is the salesperson! Now the poorly trained customer has to figure out who the buyer is. Then to make matters worse, the customer is "who" has to do the work once they find one. What does a committed salesperson do differently?

"Who's next in your family to get a car, and what's the best way for me to get ahold of them to schedule a call?"

Here's how a frustrated and uncommitted manager avoids the "who," circumventing commitment while creating vagueness during a sales meeting.

"Why aren't you guys doing what I told you!? You know (insert activity) is part of what it takes to sell cars!"

Very seldom do blanket statements apply to everyone on a team, and mass punishment erodes trust. If you want to maximize motivation, get buy-in, and drive more significant results, you'll need to take a different route because a manager needs each player to respect each other for their competency. By the same token, the team must recognize the competency of the manager leading the team. How competent is a manager who is always yelling at their employees about how incompetent the employees are?

When the manager isn't specific about "who" needs to improve, they are correcting with ambiguity and won't change anything because there's no commitment from the manager. This corrective growth opportunity has simply become a complaint session.

Let's talk about the "what".

Commitment around "what" can be a powerful tool in a conversation. A culture that lacks commitment seeks every opportunity to do as little as possible, just enough to get by. Let's think about the cost of this in the modern-day marketplace. For the "what" example, let's use a customer service example. From one to five stars, what are your customer's expectations of service? Most people say FIVE. In reality, if you just meet their minimum expectation, which is five-star service, how well do you stand out? To make the impact necessary to get the transaction and create a loyal advocate for your business, you'll need more commitment than the bare minimum.

How does a salesperson who avoids the "what" sound? Take this uncommitted reaction to their manager's request around prospecting to generate their own business.

"It's the dealership's job to bring in business, not mine." OR "I'll think about doing that." OR "Yeah I need to do something about that sometime."

The first example is blatantly committed to doing nothing, the second has committed to nothing, and the third is stating that they don't have a plan to address the issue and likely won't. In reality, the only thing we can be clear on here is that there are no "what's" clarified. With no "what," we do not have commitment.

Revisiting the non-committal sales manager avoiding the "what's" may sound like this.

"You should be (insert activity)." "You need to (insert activity)." "You need to start (insert activity)." End dialogue.

Exactly "what" are YOU going to do here, Mr./Mrs. Manager? We just don't know. My guess would be to say the same things again after a few months.

The shrewdest of the non-committals take advantage of the law of diminishing intent. The law states that the longer someone waits to do something that they know they should do, the lower the likelihood becomes that it will get done.

Enter the "when" aversion.

Let's go back to the ambiguous referral ask by our commitment lacking salesperson, note the use of the word "If" instead of "When".

"IF you meet someone who needs a car, please send them to me."

Now, the uncommitted manager and equally uncommitted employee have had an uncommitted interaction.

Manager: "Hey, you, let's get those past due CRM tasks done."

Employee: "I'll get to it when I have time, Boss."

Manager: "Okay..."

We can see in this all-too-common interaction that the employee has not committed to when they start or complete the activity. They gave a conditional response. Should they have time, only then will it happen.

Unfortunately, the problem perpetuates because the manager hasn't committed to the employee, or the accountability it takes to lock in time-framed expectations.

Words Matter

When it comes to coaching, every single word carries a lot of weight. The words you say have profound implications on your level of commitment. The words your clients say predict the future. Listen closely to the language of the person you are coaching. Reflect on your language. If you're a leader, eliminate these non-committal words and phrases from your vocabulary. When someone you're coaching uses them, challenge them directly with a coaching question.

"I may…"
(It means you probably won't.)
Challenge question: "What is getting in your way of committing to that right now?"

"I'll think about…"
(Means in the future, you will think. This couldn't be further from taking action.)
Challenge question: "If you did think about it, and had to make a decision right now, what would the decision be and why?"

"Sometime soon I'll…"
(Does "soon" mean the same thing to you as it does to me? To me, it means ten years from now.)
Challenge question: "When you say soon, when specifically will you start doing that, and have it done by?"

"Maybe…"
(Am I better off trying to get rich betting at the roulette table?)
Challenge question: "What would give you certainty here?"

"I should…"
(But you won't, because when you should-on yourself, you'd rather self-shame and accept defeat than take action.)

Chapter 5: The First Type of Coaching: Aspirational Coaching

Challenge question: "What's stopping you from turning that 'I should' into an 'I will'"?

"I might…"
(I won't hold my breath.)
Challenge question: "When you say might, it sounds like you're undecided. Where is your uncertainty coming from around that?"

"I hope that I can…"
(Hope in one hand, doodoo in the other, which one gets filled first?)
Challenge question: "Wishful thinking is one thing, what questions could you ask or decisions do you need to make to replace hope with confidence and certainty?"

"I'll try…"
(In the words of Master Yoda, "There is no try, only do.")
When you say "try", what would stop you from doing?
"One day…"
(Procrastination.)
Challenge question: "What day?"

"I will if they…"
(Means action only happens based on a contingency.)
Challenge question: "How could tying your actions (one of the few things you have control over) to other people's actions (something you can only influence), affect your success here?"

Modeling Commitment

Employees will behave in the way they see their managers act. If you're a manager and want committed employees, then the commitment must start with you. They don't see commitment when the entire action plan is solely on their shoulders. They don't take ownership when everything is always their fault. They don't feel obligated when there is no deadline or scheduled follow-up for accountability from their manager.

Change "Make more calls" into "Who will you call today, and do you know where to find them in the CRM?"

Change "You need to set appointments" into "How many appointments are you trying to set today? Who will you be calling? What coaching, scripts, or training do you need from me to achieve that goal?"

Change "You should post on social media" into "Let's stretch our comfort zones today and make some social media content together. What will we post today that will help us grow?"

Change "Do your CRM tasks" into "What's getting in the way of you getting caught up in your CRM tasks? When will you be caught up on those? How do you want me to hold you accountable for that?"

Change "Start asking for referrals" into "Walk me through your referral ask process so we can come up with ways to make it more effective right away."

Once you start taking your commitment and that of your employees, to this level, you will realize they're never lazy, unmotivated, or in a slump. They simply may fear change, don't have the ability to do what you ask, or don't see the value in doing it. These true hidden barriers only become visible when the ambiguity is challenged directly, with clarity and commitment.

Instead, seek truth and bolster commitment with collaborative discussions where co-creating action plans are the norm. Remove ambiguity, have honest, positive, impactful dialogue, create committed employees by committing to them with your effort and energy. This will help you ensure those straining, stressful, draining dialogues vanish. You will find commitment removes anger, frustration, fear, and generates momentum because there's mutual buy-in and less costly assumptions. This level of commitment always leads to trust, competency, ownership, and a mindset of accountability. And think of it like this, a business's only job is to make commitments and then meet them. If that isn't happening from you, it won't happen inside the culture of your business. If that's the case, then how can it happen on the outside, with your customers?

Create clarity and commitment by ensuring everyone knows who, does what, by when. Know that commitment is greater when both imparted from the coach with questions and the coach is part of the commitment.

Here are some of my favorite action plan and accountability questions:

- After this discussion, what's your game plan moving forward?
- When can you commit to starting that and having it done by?
- How can I be your accountability partner in this plan?
- How do you want me to approach you, if you don't meet these commitments?
- What else are you planning to do?
- (If their action plan isn't going to get the job done) I'm not sure that alone is going to get it done. What else could you do?
- When do you want me to check in to see progress here?

C - Confirm the Value of Coaching: Did they Get what they Wanted?

This is one of the most underrated steps of a coaching conversation. The value of this step is three-fold. First, ensure that the person you are coaching is happy about the tools they received from the conversation. Remember, coaching is for them not you! Thus, if they didn't receive what they wanted and needed from the conversation, your work isn't finished.

The second goal is to reinforce what was learned while checking for understanding. This principle is known as double loop learning.

Double loop learning reinforces lessons by connecting new neural pathways formed by learning something new.

In addition to reinforcing the lesson learned, confirming the value also achieves the final and most subtle of the three goals by reinforcing that coaching is valuable for the coachee while generating confidence for the coach. This completes a habit loop which duplicates the habit loop for coaching. When someone actively thinks about the value received, then communicates that value to the coach, they are creating a very rewarding physiological payout for both themselves and the coach in the form of dopamine. This dopamine chemical payout is one third of what it takes to form a habit. And what better habit to form than one of consistent ongoing continuous improvement through coaching?

Here are my favorite value building confirmation questions to ask that will achieve all three goals above:

- What are your biggest take-a-ways from today's coaching conversations?
- How will what you've gained today impact your results?
- What's different moving forward?
- What else do we need to accomplish today?
- With your new strategy, what results do you expect to see?
- How did we accomplish the goals of our conversation today?
- When you impart these new mindsets, what's different for you now?
- What growth from today will help you achieve what you want most?
- What value did you receive from coaching together here?

- What will you use and when will you use it?
- Why was today's conversation what you needed most?
- With this plan, when will you accomplish your goal?

You can test this theory with the following ACTIVITY. As you read the actual recorded responses from actual coaching clients from real coaching conversations below when conducting the Confirmation of Value Answers below, imagine that you are just finishing an effective and energizing coaching conversation with one of your direct reports. Imagine you've asked any of the questions above to your employee to confirm the value of coaching, and they look you in the eye and authentically and thoughtfully reply with any of the following claims.

"When I talk to you, I believe anything is possible. Thank you for giving me the confidence I need to grow my career."

"I think this plan is going to double my closing percentage while helping me work more efficiently with my customers without losing client satisfaction scores. This could equate to the greatest pay raise I've had in my 20-year professional career."

"I will be able to have a much better relationship with my CEO because I will be more self-aware to how I react when she's telling me uncomfortable truths. I'm going to take those truths as her wanting me to succeed rather than as an attack. As a result, our communication is going to be positive and effective on a whole new level."

"What else do we need to accomplish today? NOTHING! We've taken my biggest problem, one I've struggled with for years, and you have given me a new way to look at business and life. I think this new mindset will forever ensure I love my career here."

"I had no clue people were selling that way, and with these new talk tracks I think my profit goals and sales volume will be crushed before month end."

"This helped me realize how important personal growth and knowledge is toward getting what I want in business. I'm going to learn so much from listening to audio books daily on how to be a better salesperson. I can't believe I haven't read a book in ten years!"

"I'm going to use ALL of it! Everything we talked about from the video in my CRM to engage customers online, the names in the subject lines to increase replies from customers, the call to action at the end of the messages, funneling into appointments, and the F.U.G.I. factor to create urgency. I wouldn't be surprised if my internet closing ratio hits 25% and I become the top salesperson at the store."

"I needed a better way to have those difficult conversations with my employees and now I have that strategy. I'm so glad you helped me realize that 'sandwiching' is ineffective and does more harm than good. I can't believe I've been doing it wrong my entire career! Thank you so much!"

"I hate when you ask me 'What is your biggest take-away' because everything we talk about is a big take-away. There's always more than one!"

Pretty powerful stuff, and all real answers I've gotten when confirming the value of coaching. It's important that the coachee receives value from the coaching experience. That will keep them invested in the process. Equally important: getting affirmation of what's working for them and why helps you as the coach ensure that their needs in this area are being met.

C - Care for the Plan Long Term

It was the end of the month, and there were two different sales managers at two different Ford dealerships in the same market, who both missed their monthly quota. One was a manager, the other a coach leader. Each sales manager was having a meeting with their team. The first was the manager, shocked and livid that his team failed to perform the prior month. They had missed their goals by 40%. He yelled at his failing and disengaged employees, "I can't believe you missed the goal by 40%, it was a long month, and Ford had huge incentives. Did you even try!? You people are just lazy and that's why we were in last place in our market!"

The second was the coach leader. This sales manager was grateful and understanding. His meeting sounded like this, "One week into the month when we were reviewing sales pacing together, we realized something was off. We realized that even though we had

Chapter 5: The First Type of Coaching: Aspirational Coaching 143

huge incentives, General Motors incentives made ours look like peanuts. So, you all committed to doubling your call volume, and prospecting to our loyal owner base. You made more than twice as many calls each week for the rest of the month. As a result, we only missed our goal by 10%. We also happened to outsell every Ford store in our market. Thank you for your ideas, efforts, and open collaboration."

Both managers had the same incentives, both managers were selling the same product in the same market, both managers set goals, both managers had team meetings, both managers were communicating the outcome to their team. The differences between the manager and the coach leader follow: Managers give results reviews after it's too late to impact the outcome. Managers make assumptions while placing blame on their team. The first team wasn't lazy; they just didn't have a coach leader. Coach leaders check-in, seek to understand the situation, and collaborate throughout the journey, thus influencing the outcome. Leaders aren't surprised when results don't end up where they want them; they expect it. They have already co-created a plan, checked in on that plan throughout the process, and held their people accountable to the plan and process, not the result.

Even though no one step in D.R.I.V.E.C3™ is greater than the sum of the whole, this last step is where leaders set themselves apart from managers when it relates to effective coaching. Up until this step, every part of your coaching conversation has been the front-loaded discussion with the employee. Holding these discussions can certainly be a challenge in their own right. This is partially because you are learning an entirely new way of communicating with the leadership language of coaching and also because there is time and commitment from both the manager giving and the employee receiving coaching. Now, for the greatest challenge as it relates to coaching! Caring for the plan long term. It's not easy to have dozens of coaching conversations each week with direct reports, each creating its own action plan, and then caring for each of those plans long term!

Let's do the math on this. If you have seven direct reports that you will be coaching as part of your routine, and you choose to leverage all four types of coaching in this book, D.R.I.V.E.C3™ monthly, A.B.C., Metric Coaching bi-monthly, Observational Coaching weekly, and E.E.T.C (Expectation Exceeding Turn-around Coaching) as needed 15% of the time (one employee per month), then this would be a total of 53 coaching conversations per month, resulting in 53 different action plans. If 80% of the time these plans require accountability (measurement), then that requires 42 action plan check-ins. These 42 check-ins will often require additional coaching around barriers and obstacles that come up with new strategies, training to fill the gaps coaching uncovers, and celebrations (reward and recognition) for coaching wins. Some "care" necessary to achieve the desired results may even carry on for months or indefinitely! This portion of the chapter will cover WHY it's important and the benefits for both the leader coaching and the employee in ensuring this step is part of your process. We will also discuss how you weave this into your coaching conversation.

"The weakest pencil is better than the strongest mind."

This is why every coaching conversation can and should be documented. When consistently developing your people, you need to be consistent in the systems and processes used to document your coaching conversations. When I first started coaching, I used Microsoft "One Note," and I had a "digital coaching notebook" within one note. In that digital coaching notebook, I had a folder for each employee on my team, about twenty in total. Within each employee's folder was their quarterly goal section, and their coaching section.

I used to use my "reminders" app on my phone to remind me to check in with action plans. At some point, I started using Alexa because I enjoyed voicing the command to her rather than typing it into my phone. It was slightly more convenient. That was when I only had 50 or so to check in on each month. Currently, I use high end project management software and integrations to check in on over five hundred individual and team coaching action plans per month. That's just mine, not counting the team of coaches on my bench. Regardless of your system for documenting, following up, and checking in, what's important is you have one that is consistent and that works for you.

The Check-In Game Changer

During my stay in Iraq, insurgents attempting to hinder coalition forces by stirring up political and economic unrest decided that they could accomplish this objective by lighting the desert on fire. In order to light the desert on fire, they needed three things: heat, fuel, and oxygen. There was a massive sulfur mine in northern Iraq that would provide the fuel they needed. One day, they accomplished their goal and were able to ignite the volatile element. The fire grew so large that the smoke plume could be seen from space, and this became the largest and longest burning sulfur fire in recorded history. In fact, the fire was lit June 24, 2003, and burned for three weeks dumping 21,000 tons of sulfur dioxide into the air per day at its peak.

Our base just so happened to be downwind from this fire, and as a result we found ourselves constantly covered in a billowing smoke that hung in the air so thickly you could look directly at the desert sun with your bare eyes and just barely see a faint orange ball in the sky. We would wear our military grade gas masks 24 hours a day while living and operating in the plume. The smell of burning matches permeated our clothing and a few weeks into the fire, my entire body broke out in a rash that looked and felt like the chicken pox I had as a child. This fire had a massive impact on our mission, our enemies' mission, the region, and even affected the rest of the globe. The military, army core of engineers, and Iraqi community were dumping hundreds, if not thousands, of dump trucks worth of sand and dirt on the fire each day for days upon days before the fire went out. The reason it took so long to snuff out the flames? The fire had turned into an inferno.

The opposite of this real-life situation is a story best described in the book *To Build a Fire* written by Jack London. The story is about a frontiersman prospecting for gold in the frozen Yukon, who is in the process of freezing to death after falling into frigid water on a day when the temperature drops to seventy-five degrees below zero. As his hands begin to freeze over, and he begins to enter hypothermia, he is able to convert one match into a small flame in some kindling. Just as the kindling begins to ignite some sticks, and he begins to feel the warmth of the flame something happens. A snow-covered branch on the pine tree he mistakenly chose to start his fire under bends under the weight of the snow. It falls down through the tree and lands on his fire, extinguishing the flame; thus, causing the protagonist of the story to freeze to death.

What do these two opposite situations teach us, and what does it have to do with "Caring" for the plan you ask? First, that it's easy for a small flickering flame to go out, yet it takes extreme effort to stop the momentum of a blazing inferno. When you conduct your initial coaching conversations, you are starting a small flickering flame within the person you're coaching. This flame may be easily extinguished by external or internal factors such as: something else came up and they failed to execute, they failed to schedule it into their routine, the plan didn't work the first try and they immediately went back to the old way, etc. When you as the leader care for the plan long term, it's this additional commitment from the leader coach that converts that vulnerable flame into a burning torch of light that has the greatest positive impact on the person you're coaching and their results. This care ensures the effort you're placing on your coaching conversations drives positive change and growth for your people, your customers, and your business. Just like the raging sulfur fire, the impact of the "Care" step is more profound than words may be able to describe in this book.

Managers start a flame *under* people, one that is easily blown out without the care needed for it to grow. Leaders start a flame of purpose *within* their people, stoke that flame until it's a burning torch of confidence, lighting their individual team member's path with clarity, and fuel their momentum with accountability.

A scary coaching question: What lessons are your people learning from their new experiences?

In the section on confirming the value of coaching, we discussed "double loop learning" and its benefits where the new knowledge gained from coaching is reinforced when the person receiving coaching thinks about and proclaims this new knowledge out loud. Now it's time to bring up "Triple Loop Learning". This third loop comes afterward, when the knowledge is applied in a real-world experience and then reflected upon. It is subtly important that this reflection becomes an open dialogue between the employee and the coach during a scheduled check-in conversation.

Here's why: people's personal beliefs are shaped by the perceived results of their experiences. These beliefs are the "lessons" learned from trying something new. Trying something new is often the result of a coaching conversation. When trying something new, this is when people go from unconsciously incompetent, they don't know what they don't know, to being consciously incompetent. When someone becomes consciously incompetent, now they know what they don't know. They find out they don't know how to do it because they often fail at it the first time. Depending on the new skill being applied and the person applying said skill, it may take a lot of practice, repetition, and persistence to take that new action past conscious incompetence and into the realm of conscious competence.

On top of that, even if someone applies a new skill flawlessly, if applied to a situation of influence such as a sales interaction with a customer, there is no guarantee it will work. The danger lies in the lesson the employee learns from the outcome. It can take a lot of will and a big stretch of the comfort zone to get someone to try something. When they do, if the experience and/or result is a negative one, they may learn a negative lesson. As a result, people give up way too soon. One example of a negative lesson would be, "It doesn't work".

This negative lesson can stop the growth in its tracks, which prevents the new action plan coached on from becoming long-term behavior. As people, we often take the path of least resistance. When making change, we get that brief dip in success, and it's often easier to go back to the old way of doing things than it is to continue to fail forward until we become consciously competent. This is yet another reason why the "check-in" after a coaching conversation is critical. It gives the coaching leader a chance to address any negative outcomes and limiting beliefs that stemmed from those.

This is where checking in on the action plan to determine what perceived result occurred and the lessons from trying something new comes in. When checking in, you are curiously looking to answer the following questions:

Did they do it?
If yes, then find out how it worked for them.
If no, what got in the way? Coach them on this. Increase reward and consequence.

Did they do it properly/the best way?
If yes, then find out how many/much they did it.
If no, what could they do better next time?
Train/Roleplay/Coach on it.

Did they do it enough to produce the desired outcome?
If yes, CELEBRATE THE COACHING WIN! Document the coaching win. Reinforce with the 3-step recognition process! Create additional accountability and check in as necessary. You can raise the value of a coaching win with permission to share the success story with the rest of your team.

If not, are they going to keep trying it?
If yes, rebuild confidence and try to improve their approach; schedule next check in!

If no, what's getting in the way? Limiting beliefs: Fear, Low Value, Lack of Ability? Coach them on this. Have them re-commit to the plan, create a new/better plan, and create accountability/and or follow up. This is time for observational coaching, outlined in chapter 7, to clearly assess what's really going on.

Why CARE for the plan is so important: this one step is the back-end on employees' behavioral change and growth. It's where the up-front investment of time can pay out dividends. It's the second half of the movie where you get to see the fairy tale ending. When there isn't a fairy tale ending, this is when you find out additional barriers that are hiding in your blind spots. It's where you get to raise everyone's perception of the value you bring as a leader. It's where you get to solidify your brand as someone who commits, executes, and follows through. It's where you get to build trust between you and your people as a leader. This is when that small spark in a bundle of kindling ignites into that burning torch of light that fuels momentum and growth.

Let me give you an example of a recent "Care" step that made a massive positive impact for a sales professional I coach because everything worked out. Then, in the coaching around limiting beliefs section, I will give you another with a manager, where it didn't and how this step made a massive positive impact for both him and my company.

D.R.I.V.E.C3™ Coaching Convo Start to Finish

At the time of writing this book, I have been blessed to coach with some of the top sales professionals at the top automotive dealerships in the nation. Alabama coach Nick Saben and his automotive business partner Joe Agresti, owners of Dream Motor Group, a highline store selling mostly rare Mercedes-Benz vehicles, invest in their managers and employees with coaching. Employees at businesses like this are often extremely talented, driven to succeed, and value personal growth and ongoing continuous improvement. As such, I was giving a coaching conversation to one of the group's top Mercedes-Benz sales professionals, named Bea, in Dream Motor group.

Did they do it?

If YES,
find out how it worked for them!

If NO,
Find out what got in the way?
Coach them on this!
Increase reward & consequence.

Did they do it properly / the best way?

If YES,
then find out how much / how many they did.

If NO,
What could they have done better next time? Role play, train, coach on it!

Did they do it enough to produce the desired outcome?

If YES,
CELEBRATE THE COACHING WIN!
Document the coaching win.
Reinforce with 3 step recognition process.

Are they going to keep trying it?

If YES,
rebuild their confidence!
Try to improve their approach!
Schedule next check in.

If NO,
What's getting in the way?
Limiting Beliefs: Fear, Low Value, Lack of Ability?
Coach them on this! This is the time for observational coaching!.

Chapter 5: The First Type of Coaching: Aspirational Coaching

Bea is a 20-year automotive sales veteran. Almost like clockwork, each month Bea finds more business for her dealer group from her social media presence, relentless prospecting efforts, and the amazing experience she gives her customers, yet Bea still values ongoing development and coaching.

At the time, one of Bea's areas of opportunity to improve was a better understanding of the reporting her dealership uses and the ability to turn the data into actionable areas to improve.

The following is an example of her coaching conversation and the "Care" for the plan where the check-ins led to good lessons with the desired outcome using the flowchart above.

"Bea, what I want for you is that you are able to use the reporting to make a positive impact in your goals and success. Is now a good time to have our coaching conversation?" I recruited Bea to our convo and asked permission to kick off our coaching session.

Bea warmly smiled and replied with her thick German accent, "Sure! Just know when I look at the report and I see all the numbers and all the red boxes it looks negative and makes me feel like I am failing."

Grateful she outlined that obstacle up front and wanting to make sure we addressed that during our coaching I asked, "What would it mean for you if by the end of our coaching you could view the data and reporting as a positive because it helped you move toward your goals?"

"That would be amazing, and if anyone can help me overcome this it's you with your approach." She verified that she was open to tackling that together.

With the green light, I proceeded to point out what could be an area of opportunity within the report, "Bea, check out the correlation between customers with whom you conduct a proposal and your closing ratio. What are you seeing here?"

"It looks like whoever I propose ends up taking a Mercedes home!" She smiled.

I nodded because that was what I noticed as well, "Now look at the proposal to visit ratio, what do you see here?"

"It looks like I'm proposing about 23% of my visits," she read from the report.

I wanted to discover the value that she could gain from today's convo and align our coaching efforts around a key area that would make a positive impact for her, "Correct, and you close almost all of those. In this conversation, if we could help you increase your proposal percentage, would that make this convo valuable for you?"

She laughed and smiled, "Yes, because then I will easily sell more cars!"

We were clearly aligned to the objectives of the convo, and there was buy-in from the recruitment. Now, it was time to move into the Inquiry stage of coaching, "Let's discuss the other 77% of customers who don't end up getting a proposal. When you don't end up giving them a proposal, what gets in the way?"

"I don't give people a proposal who aren't ready to buy a car," Bea replied calmly.

"How do you know someone isn't ready to buy a car?" I asked.

Bea stated, "When the customer tells me, 'This is our first stop.' Or 'We're not planning on buying anything today,' then I know they aren't ready to buy."

Chapter 5: The First Type of Coaching: Aspirational Coaching

"When in your sales process does the customer tell you that Bea?" I needed more details before I could even think about verifying the gap I was beginning to uncover, so I continued inquiring.

Bea thought about it for a moment and replied, "Usually right off the bat. Yes, they tell me that when I go meet them on the lot, or right after they sit down at my desk."

In the automotive industry, sometimes this customer response stems from a fear of high-pressure salespeople. Salespeople who fear coming across as high pressure or transactional salespeople who are only looking for a quick sale today and don't value following up long-term with customers may dismiss a customer like this.

My immediate assumption with Bea was the first scenario; perhaps upon hearing this, she wouldn't continue with the sales process wanting to avoid high pressure selling situations. However, instead of reacting on that assumption and risk offending Bea, I stayed objective and asked an open-ended question, "Okay, and when a customer tells you that, then what do you do?"

"Well, I still follow the sales process. I assess their needs and wants; I find them the closest in-stock vehicle to show them. I build rapport with the customer. I pull the vehicle right up front. We walk around it, and I show them everything that matters on the vehicle, and we drive it together," she confidently replied.

Happy I didn't put my foot in my mouth by insulting this process driven sales pro with my assumption, I then asked, "And after you get back from the demo drive, then what do you do with those customers? You know, the ones who told you they weren't ready to buy today in the beginning."

"That's the point at which I give them my business card, and then I ask them when and how I should follow up. I schedule the call in the CRM and follow up when I'm supposed to."

It looked like the inquiry stage of the D.R.I.V.E.C3™ coaching process had come to an end. At this point, the missing puzzle piece I had uncovered needed to be verified before I could add value. I used a question to accomplish the "V", "For those customers, how and when do you ask for the sale?"

"I don't." Bea stated, verifying the missing puzzle piece.

Her tone changed from confidence in her process to curiosity, "Why would I ask for the sale, they already told me they weren't planning on buying today?"

Now it was time to educate Bea. It was time to help her bring forth from within the answers that would help her improve her result, receive value from our conversation, and ultimately help her look at reporting and statistics through a new positive lens.

I asked, "In your twenty-one years of selling, have you ever sold a car to someone who told you afterward, "I wasn't planning on buying today?" I questioned with 99.99% certainty this had happened because almost anyone who sells almost anything for any amount of time has heard this.

"Yes, of course!" Bea replied immediately. "In fact, a lady who bought a used car told me that just last week."

"For what reasons would a customer vocalize to you that they are 'not going to buy today'?" I educated.

Bea thought about it and replied, "Maybe because they have questions that aren't yet answered? Another reason could be that they aren't sold on the car." She stopped.

"I agree with those Bea, and it could be a knee jerk reaction out of fear. Some customers fear high pressure buying situations, and this is a defense mechanism." I added a little value.

Bea nodded in agreement.

"What does it mean for you and your customers that the following three things are possible? First, that many of the customers who told you they were 'just looking, not buying today or that they just started shopping' did so out of fear, due to unanswered questions, or because they hadn't yet decided on the vehicle? Second, that after they told you this in the onset, due to your process, ability to build trust, rapport, and value in your vehicle, you eliminated their fears, answered their questions, and helped them realize that this was the perfect vehicle for them? And third, simply because you didn't ask them if they wanted to move forward now, they didn't?" I was curious to see what her response to this question would be.

Her eyes lit up with what I can only describe as renewed determination, and she enthusiastically replied, "You're right! It would mean for me that I could help a lot more customers take their new vehicles home… It would save me a lot of time and less follow up efforts necessary…" She paused for a moment, then continued. "And for my customers, it would mean they save time. They would get to deal with me and would avoid accidentally ending up with a car salesperson who doesn't actually care about them. Wow, this is huge."

Bea had clearly been educated, and now it was time for the first C, co-create an action plan. "So, what are you going to do moving forward?" I asked.

Bea immediately replied, "I'm going to ask for the sale every time."

I smiled, knowing this could be a game changer for Bea, and how this new action was going to help her be more efficient and give her customers an even better experience. While we had coached on the what, now it was time to coach on the how. I wanted for her new activity to yield the most impactful results. I probed, "When and how will you ask for the sale?"

"I will ask immediately after the test drive. And I'll ask by saying, 'Shall we go over your finance, lease, and purchasing options now?'" she said thoughtfully.

We coached a little longer on the message she would deliver when attempting to have more customers review the proposal and asking for the sale. I shared my strategy in asking for the sale which myself and thousands of salespeople I have trained and coached have found extremely effective. (I am happy to share that with you as well—email me Sean@CarMotivators.com.)

"What percentage of the time will you ask for the sale, and when will you start?" I questioned Bea to find out if there were any last seeds of doubt, or concerns remaining.

She replied immediately and with confidence, "100% and with my next customer! Yes, this is awesome."

Now that we had co-created her action plan, it was time to confirm the value of coaching, so I asked, "What overall impact will today's conversation and the plan you created have on your statistical reporting roadblock, and, more importantly, your work satisfaction and customers' experience?"

Chapter 5: The First Type of Coaching: Aspirational Coaching

"I can tell you right off the bat, the reporting is a lot less intimidating. I think this is going to be great, and you're going to see a lot more sales out of me... and I believe I'll have happier customers, too. Thanks, Sean!" she said with deep gratitude.

The value had been confirmed, and finally it was time to set up the final C, to ensure I knew how to "Care" for the plan. I finished our convo with, "It's my absolute pleasure, Bea! And how do you want me to support your plan moving forward?"

Bea replied, "Text me once a week and see how asking for the sale is going!"

This conversation happened near the end of September, and once a week for the rest of October, I checked in with Bea on her action plan. Bea was kind enough to allow me to share the check-in convo's as well, and the results that ensued from her plan.

October 9th Text from Sean to Bea: *100%?!?*

October 14th Text from Sean to Bea: *What % are you at today Bea?* ☺

Text from Bea to Sean: *Yes! Numbers are going to increase—it becomes second nature. I am becoming more aware of the NOW moment.*

Reply to Bea from Sean: *That's awesome Bea, keep pushing!!!*

Reply from Bea to Sean: *Until it becomes this easy!* with a funny emoji of a football player knocking another down.

October 26th Text from Sean to Bea: *100% and easy yet?!*

Reply from Bea: *Yes, it is getting much easier to ask for the sale!*

Reply from Sean: *Congrats on the growth Bea! How is this making a positive impact on your results?*

Reply from Bea: *Oh Yeah!!! 75% proposal and 35%+ closing!*

Reply from Sean: *So strong! You're an inspiration, Bea! No more fear of metrics for you?*

Reply from Bea: *Not the way you used it to help me figure out where to get better. I just need you to be my metric translator! All I used to see is red and some green in those metrics and to me it meant, FAIL/pass. And all you see is where the potential is. So thank YOU.* ☺

November 1st, Text from Sean to Bea: *100% in November?*

Reply from Bea: *Nearly doubled my sales last month from the previous one, and off to a good start. Lets do 100% for November!*

Chapter 5: The First Type of Coaching: Aspirational Coaching

Section 1: Sales Performance (70% of focus)

Notes:

- Showroom proposal increased was 83%
- Showroom closing was 50%
- Highest Weighted closing at 15%
- Campaign totals 22 at 25% closing
- Internet leads appointments set at 18%
- ILM closing 13.6%
- Crushed CE 100% response rate and 1,000 average score (touch wood)

Section 2: Coaching Performance Evaluation (30% of focus)

What most drives this teammate to perform at the highest level?

Positive energy and results-driven

How is my coaching helping this teammate? Include metrics as appropriate.

Stay focused, positive, disciplined, consistent and REPEAT

Aspirational coaching is a powerful tool. When you know what someone wants, then you can help them get there, just like I helped Bea. Ready to get started? Head on over to my website L2coach.com for a free PDF download of a sample aspirational coaching form.

Chapter 6

The Second Type of Coaching: Metric Coaching

D.R.I.V.E.C3™ is the foundation of coaching success which will be utilized throughout all the coaching processes discussed in this book. The second type of coaching we will cover is A.B.C. Metric Coaching. Why do I love metric coaching? Its benefits are vast and include:

- Improving performance in key areas
- Uncovering and repairing broken processes
- Zeroing in on missing best practices
- Setting and accomplishing business goals through your team members
- Improving utilization of software and tech investments
- Ability to A/B test new processes
- Easily track growth and accountability toward desired outcomes

Not sold on it yet? Let me walk you through the process and the great impact this can have for people on your team.

What I want for you in reading this portion of the book about coaching on metrics is that you learn to take a cold dead thing like numbers and stats, useless in their own right, and read them seeking to find the underlying story they tell. Then leveraging recruitment to get the buy-in around the metric coaching conversation, you will coach your team member and co-create action plans to improve the data. And that's exactly what A.B.C. Metric Coaching is—a leader's ability to A – Assess the data, B – Generate Buy-in for a coaching conversation, and C – Co-Create action plans that lead to growth. Since we've already spent a lot of time on the "Buy-in" and the "Co-Creating action plans," we can focus in on the "Assess" here.

When I was Chief Business Development Officer of DriveCentric CRM, I was able to have engagements with managers across the automotive industry and tech companies spanning into other verticals as well. At one point, our goal was to determine which modules, features, and benefits in a robust CRM system would be best to present if given the opportunity to give a ten-minute software demo. We simply couldn't cover everything in that short amount of time! I did some one-on-one interviews with a couple hundred managers, and one area I dug into was reporting and metrics, trying to figure out if reporting and data were worth focusing much on during presentations.

What I found was that fewer than 15% of managers conducted regular metric coaching conversations with their employees. Of the businesses interviewed, fewer than 50% of the employees who did receive "coaching" on the data felt as if the metrics helped them grow. Of those employees who did see value in the metrics, fewer than 20% of those walked away from those conversations with actionable plans to implement, follow up, accountability, reward, and recognition for growth from those conversations.

Do the math on this... 15% of managers give metric coaching < 50% employees received value < 20% had a plan, accountability and wins/challenges... 100 x 15% = 15... 15 x 50% = 7.5... 7.5 x 20% =

Chapter 6: The Second Type of Coaching: Metric Coaching

1.5 That's right! This means fewer than 2% of employees likely receive effective coaching by their standard (and mine).

When I took over the dealership, it was already a great team. The dealership was the number 1 Hyundai dealership in the St. Louis district month after month for several consecutive years. Out of about 13 dealerships, they were always number one. Some would argue, due to diminishing returns, it's harder to get growth from a high producer. When it came to regional stats, the dealership had never finished number one. In fact, the dealership was almost always between 50th place, and 150th out of 200 or so dealerships. I remember the first time my store had a first-time regional finish, and we did it while completely eliminating our radio ad marketing budget. I told the owners of our company, get rid of the marketing spend—we don't need it. Our people and inventory are all we need to grow.

That confidence came from the skilled, motivated, purpose-driven team we had developed through coaching. On top of that first time regional finish, we were the only Hyundai store up in a down market. For two years, the St. Louis market was down year over year, but not our store. We were capturing market share and increasing sales volume, gross profit, and net profit on both new and pre-owned vehicles. One of the owners asked me how. My reply was, "Coaching." Here's how to enact A.B.C. Metric Coaching to grow your results. A great book on metrics is *KPI Checklists* by Bernie Smith.

As it relates to metrics, there are many limiting beliefs that create barriers to good metric coaching. Some of them I'm sure you're familiar with, such as, the data isn't accurate, it's not fair to compare us to other stores, or compare me to other salespeople. And as a result of these limiting beliefs, people either avoid convos involving metrics altogether, or they discredit and resist them. It's crucial to address these beliefs and help individuals overcome them.

By understanding two things, you can overcome these limiting mindsets. First, you must understand that the goal of ABC Metric coaching is simply to use the data to identify who coaching with and what specific area will have the biggest gains in the shortest time.

Second, coaching in general is the cycle of continuous, never-ending improvement, regardless of what the metrics say, or the disparity of accuracy. It's still important and impactful to seek measurable opportunities for growth in the data, and then pour into your people.

To conduct effective metric coaching, you must first assess the data to find the greatest opportunities. Do this by simply comparing VOLUME metrics to PERFORMANCE metrics. When it comes to analyzing metrics, the key lies in identifying the areas of low performance with high volume and high performance with low volume. These points of disparity provide valuable coaching opportunities. There may be a tendency to overlook coaching opportunities for top-performing salespeople because they already achieve satisfactory results. However, metric coaching allows even top producers to enhance their performance further.

You can do this as it relates to metrics centered on your entire team or on an individual's stats. Say, for example, that an entire team's sales stats show a high volume of internet leads with a low closing %. This is a perfect opportunity to coach the team members to make a big impact by bringing that % up.

We can also look at the opposite. You might have a salesman, Keith, who has a high closing percentage on the phone but has a low volume of opportunity. This would definitely create a coaching opportunity aiming to help this sales consultant get more inbound sales calls.

After assessing the data, now you will get buy-in using a recruitment statement. Let's say Keith wants to buy his girlfriend a really nice engagement ring. You see that if he were to take more phone calls, he could easily sell a few more cars per month, which would fund his lady's diamond ring.

A recruitment statement might sound like this, "Joe, what I want for you is that you're able to get the nicest possible ring for your girlfriend. After looking at some reports, I found some areas to make that happen! Is now a good time to discuss how?"

Finally, conduct your coaching conversation following the D.R.I.V.E.C3™ Coaching framework. The only difference here is that you will set specific metric goals with Keith, tied directly to the stats you're wanting to help him improve. For the example here, you may consider asking a question like, "After this convo, how many sales calls do you want to set a goal to take before this month is over?" to set those clear goals.

Remember this, software programs need metrics, and people need coaching. Don't use metrics to browbeat, embarrass, or belittle the people on your team. Instead, use the A.B.C.'s of Metric Coaching to identify your greatest opportunities for growth and hone in on improving key players with positive and impactful metric coaching.

Since many people don't understand their metrics or are too afraid to look at them, without coaching the tendency is to ignore them. It's not that people don't want to improve, but something is stopping them. There are three main obstacles that keep someone from taking action on something:

Don't See Value
Don't Know How
Fear

These are what you need to address. For Keith he can see the value because he wants that diamond ring for his girlfriend. He just needed a higher volume to get there since his closing percentage was already good.

For some salesmen, there is a fundamental lack of understanding of how to do something. Coaching helps with that as well. You can introduce them to the best practices of your high closers. Another approach is to ask them specific questions about their performance. For example, where do you feel your process is getting stuck? How would you rate yourself on your ability to handle warranty issues? Or in Keith's case, "What's stopping you from taking more inbound sales calls?"

By encouraging self-assessment, we allow individuals to identify their areas of improvement based on the metrics. Instead of simply pointing out what needs to be better, we guide them through a process of self-reflection and help them come up with strategies to enhance their performance. This approach shifts the conversation and fosters a more constructive coaching experience.

Some people have a basic fear of the numbers or of change or how to implement it. Limiting beliefs often play a factor in this, and addressing the underlying problem can help. Also focusing on the attitudes behind the metrics and not on the numbers themselves can be key.

I made significant strides with the St. Louis dealership when we implemented something that had never been done before. It was a major win for us. Previously, I used to look at CRM and sales metrics from a holistic perspective. I would evaluate closing percentages for all salespeople and determine if they were good or not. However, I realized the importance of diving deeper into those metrics. I started segmenting the closing percentages based on different types of sales. For example, the skills required to close an internet customer or upsell an inbound phone call are different from those needed to sell to a campaign customer and a dealership location walk-in. This provides different coaching opportunities.

During one of my coaching sessions, I was discussing closing percentage with a salesperson. I expected them to express a desire for more internet leads, but to my surprise, they said they didn't want them. I was taken aback by their response and asked for clarification. The salesperson explained that they disliked internet leads and had no interest in working with them. They preferred to focus on other lead sources where they excelled and were more comfortable.

While it may seem unconventional or counterproductive, I chose to respect the salesperson's preference and led them in the way they wanted to be led. I turned off their internet leads, which made them happier, and in turn, our overall performance improved.

Sometimes, it's important to recognize when a square peg doesn't fit in a round hole.

Information is powerful and numbers are important. Understanding what's behind the numbers is even more crucial. Ready to get started? Head on over to my website L2coach.com for a free PDF download of a sample metrics coaching form.

Chapter 7

The Third Type of Coaching: Observational Coaching

Before we talk about observational coaching, I want to ask you a couple quick questions. Do you consider yourself a professional in your field? It's a yes or no question, don't overthink it! What about the individuals on your team, are they professionals?

Observational coaching is deeply ingrained in our society with sports and athletics. Think about it. What professional athlete doesn't have a coach on the sidelines watching them practice or play the game and giving them input on how they can improve? That's exactly what observational coaching entails. Except instead of watching the players on your team swing the bat, run the bases, and field the ball, you're observing each person on your team as they conduct each step in their sales process.

Most of the time at dealerships, we observe the proposal presentation and negotiation step. That's great, but what about the online customer experience, owner base mining, lead handling, the greeting, needs assessment, walk around presentation, trade valuation, demo drive, service introduction, and memorable digital delivery? By imparting observational coaching in your leadership routine, you will be able to pinpoint training opportunities and transfer the right skills to the right people. This will help them master what they need to get even better results.

When it comes to employees being observed, they often feel like they're being attacked and criticized. When that happens, they stop listening. Instead, they go on the defensive and they start coming up with excuses. What we need to do is articulate a process for observational coaching so the employee knows that we're going to talk about the bad and the good, and then there's going to be a collaborative effort to improve moving forward. That's when observational coaching becomes extremely valuable.

For a moment, think about taking a commercial airline flight. What makes us feel okay about letting someone, a pilot, fly us across the country? We know that they've been trained and tested for competency. They've done book tests, and they've been observed flying the plane by someone else who is an experienced pilot.

Think about the last time you or a loved one needed surgery. What makes us feel okay about letting someone operate on us? We know they've gone to school, they've been trained, and they've been tested for competency. Before they could operate on real patients, someone else who knows what they're doing has even observed them conducting practice surgery. Be thankful this is the case! While I am not a doctor myself, or anything close to it, I did take a three day "combat lifesaver course" in the Army. Part of the course was to learn to give IV fluids. We had to practice on fake arms, then eventually practice on our fellow classmates. My high school friend and platoon mate Sergeant Lance Coffman was my combat life saver battle buddy, and even with a seasoned combat medic giving him observational coaching, it still took him five tries to get the IV drip going in my arm! I'm hoping to forgive him one day!

Before I understood coaching and training best practices, one of the biggest mistakes I would make as a manager was telling people how to do something and then just assuming they knew how to do it and would do it the way I taught them. Well, we know that to assume something makes an "ass" out of "u" and "me".

We have to stop assuming, even for our top producing salespeople, that they're doing everything perfectly. We need to pretend like our salespeople are the pilots flying the plane of our company's success across the country. We need to treat our managers as if they are the doctors operating on our loved ones, our employees, and customers. We need to be 100% certain that they are competent in every step in our sales process, and then continue to sharpen that edge. To achieve that level of trust is where observational coaching comes in.

Observational coaching is going to verify that your coachee can do what you want them to do. It's going to help them to know their manager is committed to accountability around their processes and expectations. It's also going to help you as the coach identify how they can do it even better so that you may transfer the right skills. The difference between success and failure in a sale can come down to some finite nuances. It's one thing to know someone has the potential to do something better and another to know that they are going to actually do it better.

The Tools of Observational Coaching

Observational coaching has many tools at its disposal, including:

- Watching them in action and giving coaching to improve.
- Roleplaying to transfer skills and help others improve.
- Uncovering blind spots and improving top performers.
- Removing bad habits in veteran employees.

- Ensuring expectations are being met.

Watching them in Action and Giving Coaching to Improve

Observational coaching is fundamentally watching your sales consultant doing part of their job and then giving them coaching to improve that area. Whether its customer greeting, asking for the sale, closing, handling incoming calls or internet leads, or anything else related to their job, you can observe them doing it and find ways to help them enhance their performance.

You can do observational coaching on any area of performance, even if its something that the employee is already good at. After all, there are always ways to improve! You can help them become good at the things they're bad at and great at the things they're good at. The goal is to constantly be improving.

Watching them in real-life interactions is extremely helpful. You can train people to do certain processes or about company best practices. They can even recite procedures and policies back to you. Until you see real-world interactions, though, you don't know if they're actually doing what they've been trained to do.

Roleplaying to Transfer Skills and Help Others Improve

Roleplaying can be a crucial piece of the puzzle for observational training. While not everyone will have experience roleplaying, or be comfortable with it, it can help anyone improve and get practice in key areas before trying their new processes out on customers. By playing the customer, you can help coach your employee through the interaction, letting them become comfortable with what they're going to say or do when in front of an actual customer. You can even reverse the roles so that they are playing the customer and get a chance to see how you would handle different scenarios they throw at you.

Uncovering Blind Spots and Improving Top Performers

When observing and coaching employees, you'll find that sometimes they know instinctively when something isn't working. Other times, though, they might have no idea that there is a better way to handle something or that they're doing something the wrong way. These "blind spots" can hold back especially top performers who are doing well but don't realize that with some small changes they could be taking their sales to a whole new level.

Ensuring Expectations are Being Met

Again, you can train all you want, it doesn't mean that your employees are doing what you trained them to do in real-world encounters with customers. Through observational coaching, you can make sure that not only are they doing what they've been trained to do but also that they are upholding the company's values at the same time.

Removing Bad Habits in Veteran Employees

It's really easy to develop bad habits in our job. Take something like the road to a sale. In automotive, there's ten steps which may seem simple but can be extremely complicated when you get into the details of it. This is a prime place for bad habits to set in. An employee forgets to do things or decides that certain steps aren't valuable. Observational training is a good way to pinpoint where things have become lax or where fundamental misunderstandings have come into play.

Rules of Engagement for Observational Coaching

When conducting effective observational coaching, I recommend following three rules. It's important to balance the positives and negatives. Let them talk first. Finally, follow the KISS method and keep it simple and systematic.

Rule 1 Balance the Positives AND Negatives

During observation, it's always easier to point out the things people are messing up. That being said, in every sports game, both the winning and losing team have good and bad plays. It's important to identify both, so you can duplicate and perpetuate the good plays, while improving upon the bad ones.

Rule 2 They Get to Talk First!

Think about all the times you get something wrong and self-realize it right away! If you're like me, then you're probably your own worst critic. As such, if you are already browbeating yourself for messing something up, what value is it if your boss does the same thing? The answer is, it's not!

It's a waste of time and energy to beat a dead horse, and if you give someone something they already have, you're not adding value. So during observational coaching, you're taking notes, and you will review those areas of opportunity with them. But you'll only spend time coaching on the things that they *didn't* know they did wrong. In both leadership and sales, there are no free words.

Rule 3 Follow the KISS Method: Keep it Simple and Systematic

Don't overload the convo. You may notice fifteen things they can do better, but you're not going to point them all out. Imagine if you were to get golf lessons; your golf instructor wouldn't point out all 15 things you're doing wrong and expect you to fix every one on the next swing. Growth and skill mastery are an ongoing process, so you're just going to home in on 2 or 3 things maximum.

Steps for Effective Observational Coaching Conversations

To give an effective observational coaching convo, the following steps must be accomplished.

Preparation

First, comes the preparation. This stage shouldn't take but a few minutes. Start by choosing the specific step in your process that you want to observe for mastery. Next, review your coaching notes from the last time you observed this team member in action. What commitments did they make in their last action plan? You're going to be watching to see if they've made those changes.

Observation

Second, comes the observation itself. You will actually watch the person doing the actual step in the process with a real customer. In the event you're unable to and you need to tighten up your coaching cadence and schedule, roleplay can substitute.

As you observe them in the process, you are going to try to write down 3 things they did well that you want them to continue, and you will write down 3 things that didn't go well that they can improve upon. During this process, it's important that you don't interrupt to teach. If you do that, then this coaching convo quickly becomes a training session.

Coach

Finally, it's time to coach, co-create an action plan and commit to positive change. First, ask them what they did well. Compare their list to yours. Then re-enforce the things that were on both lists, and recognize them for the things they did well that weren't on their list.

Moving forward, they will have a better idea of how to duplicate success.

Now ask them what didn't go well that they can improve. Again, compare their list to yours. Briefly reinforce the things they think they can improve that were on both lists, but don't waste a lot of time on those. It's more important that you focus your coaching efforts on the things they didn't do well that are on your list but not theirs. I call these blind spots. By focusing on the blind spots, you're giving them new information that they didn't already have, which makes your engagement exponentially more valuable. Now that the salesperson knows what they did right and what they did wrong, it's time to co-create the action plan.

Co-Create an Action Plan

A manager teaches salesperson X the proper meet and greet. He thinks, "Okay. I taught him the meet and greet. He's good. I'm assuming he's going to use it. Two months later and salesperson X's results aren't good, and he can't get anyone on a demo drive. What does the manager say? "He should be doing it. I taught him that he should be doing a good meet and greet. He should be getting people on the demo drive, right?" The word "should" is the excrement of an assumption.

Two months of bad results with observational coaching would have eventually changed the outcome. You could ensure that he was doing what he was supposed to and see where it needs to be improved. Employees need your help through this process. One thing you have to understand, and this is huge, is experience alone is not a teacher. If it were, we'd only hire 20-year sales veterans because they'd be selling a hundred cars a month or more. The vast majority of them are not, though, because experience alone doesn't cut it. You need to know what you're doing and how to do it better. Lots of experienced salespeople and managers are stuck because they don't get the feedback they need to improve from managers, and that's because they don't give them this type of observational coaching.

Experience plus reflection creates opportunity. It's not just enough to have time in the job, you must also have reflection. This is one of the most powerful tools we have in our arsenal for personal and team development. When we really start analyzing our efforts and looking in the mirror, then we can do something about it. It creates the opportunity for growth. It doesn't make the growth happen, but it creates the opportunity. What turns the opportunity into growth is action.

We need to ensure action. How do we do that? When it comes to coaching, stop robbing your people of their ability to solve problems by giving them the answer. Too many coaches just want to jump in and give an answer, but for it to be meaningful, the answer must come from within the coachee.

One of my coaches says, "If they build it, they own it. If they own it, they'll act on it."

People are significantly more likely to act if they come up with an action plan themselves, because people aren't going to come up with an action plan they're not willing to do. This is double loop learning, when they come up with the answers. It's in their head, then they say it out loud to their coach. It's more than doubling the probability of retention.

When we give someone the answer, we rob them of the ability to solve problems. More than that, since it's our answer and not theirs, we don't know if they have the ability to implement the action plan. We don't know if they're even willing to try. The odds of their even remembering to act on it have gone down significantly since it didn't originate from inside them.

Einstein said that education is not the learning of facts, but the training of the mind to think. That's what we're doing with coaching, training our employees to think and problem solve. That's how we are educating them and creating scalability. If we give them the answer, we are not educating. We are creating dependency.

When creating the action plan, keep it simple, revolving around start, stop, and continue. Ask them after the coaching session:

- What will you **start** doing?
- What will you **stop** doing?
- What will you **continue** doing that you did well?

Once you've worked out the plan, commit to the positive change and caring for the plan.

Commit to Positive Change

Finally, commit to caring for the plan with the following question, "When should I check in to see how that's working for you?" It's not enough to just have a plan; it needs to be implemented, and, where necessary, modified. Accountability is key and is part of what's called triple loop learning.

Triple Loop Learning

Triple loop learning is where people really start to take what they've learned to heart. They have gone beyond talking about it; they're actually doing it. The action they're taking helps them understand and incorporate change more naturally into their being.

Accountability

When you check in, you're looking to see if they're following the plan and whether or not the plan is working. If they're not following it, you need to together figure out what the obstacles are. If they are following it and it's not working, you need to figure out why it's not working or what else they can do differently. If they are following the plan and it is working, then congratulations and encouragement to keep going are in order. Ask them how they want to be held accountable. See the flow chart in Chapter 5 on Aspirational Coaching.

Measured Improvement

What you're looking for at this point is measured improvement. If they are implementing the plan, is it working? How is the improvement being measured? I was coaching a salesperson named Darren who had a problem because every time a customer commented that a payment was high, he'd immediately go to his managers and ask for a discount which was hurting the bottom line. I asked him how he could weed out the people who couldn't afford the high payment from those who just were looking for a discount.

He came up with the idea of standing his ground and reiterating what a good price it actually was. Then he'd ask for the customer to sign the proposal. We agreed that I would touch base with him in two weeks. When I did I was thrilled to learn that he had stuck to his plan and had actually doubled his commissions. He stopped assuming that everyone who wanted a discount actually needed one in order to purchase and stopped automatically trying to get it for them.

Coach Around Challenges

If the plan isn't working, this is the time to coach around the challenges that have come up with the plan. These may be either in the employee's willingness to implement the plan or the plan's effectiveness. Either way there is a solution. Remember to let your employee try to find it on their own through guided questioning from you. A person is more likely to implement a plan if they feel ownership of it.

Celebrate Wins/Growth

Find out how they want to be rewarded. For some people money is the big motivator. For others they crave recognition and praise. One employee might want to be taken out to lunch and given special attention. Some might want their success to be called out in front of the entire group. Understand what motivates them and makes them feel rewarded. Then show them how by continuous improvement they can achieve more of what it is they're wanting (i.e., money, recognition, praise, helping out the team, etc.).

Many managers give recognition by saying "good job," but this is too vague because often people don't know what exactly made them succeed. If they don't know what made them succeed, how will they know to intentionally duplicate it? When giving recognition, there is a surefire way to duplicate and perpetuate desired behaviors through a four-step recognition process. Step one, explain exactly what they did well. The more specific the better. Step two, share the benefits of how it positively impacts the team and business. Step three, let them know what's in it for them if they continue the desired behaviors. Step four, simply encourage them to keep it up. In the case of Darren, it sounded like this:

"Darren, the way you have been handling price objections by holding the value of the products you're selling instead of going straight to a discount shows a vast improvement in your selling skills! The extra money you're generating for the company is making a positive impact in our marketing budget. If you continue to do that, you should continue to see a pretty big increase in your paycheck! Congrats and please keep it up!"

When you compare that four-step recognition process to "good job," you can see a big difference and why that approach will re-create success.

Cycle of Continuous Improvement

Remember, coaching isn't a one-and-done thing. It's a journey of continuous improvement through a career. The goal is to make

Chapter 7: The Third Type of Coaching: Observational Coaching

the drive to continuously improve themselves a part of the person's DNA. The more success they have in improving themselves and their skillsets, the more they're going to want. When one set of goals has been accomplished, there's always the next set of goals to create. Challenge for skill mastery with skill or process specific coaching, commit to the plan, care for the plan, rinse and repeat.

Observational Coaching Can Happen at Any Time

You'll want to schedule observational coaching sessions for all your employees, but you don't have to wait for a scheduled session to utilize this tool. I was visiting a service department, waiting to talk to someone I was going to coach, and I had an opportunity to observe Steve while I was waiting. His job was to check customers into the service department.

While I was waiting, he checked in a woman who hadn't been there for a couple of years. He gave her a friendly smile and said, "Welcome back." He then commented that she hadn't been in for a couple of years and politely asked her why.

She told him it was because there was a new service advisor there every time she came, making it hard to establish a relationship, so she'd just been going to the Jiffy Lube near her house. He accepted that answer and finished checking her in.

While I was waiting, I was also able to observe him interacting with a gentleman who was picking up his car. Steve went over with him what the car needed right then, what it would need in the near future, and what was alright and unlikely to need attention for a while. These are referred to as the red items, yellow items, and green items. While Steve mentioned a yellow item, the tires which would need to be replaced in the near future, he didn't mention a valve that was a red item and needed to be replaced immediately.

Afterward, I had an opportunity to talk to Steve one-on-one and ask him some questions about what I had observed. I started by asking him what he did well. He correctly identified that he was polite, welcoming, and prompt. We then covered what he could improve on.

With the female customer, I asked him why he didn't address why she hadn't been coming in once she told him the reason. I helped him realize that he could have volunteered to be her advisor since he'd been there for ten years. He could ask for her loyalty.

Then, we discussed the interaction with the man and the reds, yellows, and greens on the car report. He said that he felt the valve which was a red was something the car didn't really need as it could run fine without it. I helped him realize that he should let the customer know so the customer could make the decision. It makes people feel good to know they are maintaining their vehicle. I also inquired why he didn't offer to replace the tires, which were a yellow, while they already had the car, which would save the customer a return trip in a couple of months. He said there were surveys that went out and he could potentially be marked down for pushing a yellow item which he didn't want.

I asked what would be in it for the customer to offer to handle it that day. Steve correctly came to the conclusion that not only would it save the customer time in the long run but also potentially money since they were at that time running a special on tires which might not be the case when the tires became a "must fix today" issue.

I asked Steve what he was going to start doing, stop doing, and continue doing. He said he was going to start asking them to take care of the yellow, stop assuming they don't want certain repairs, and continue putting the customer first.

That one conversation from a non-scheduled observation radically changed things for Steve. The department's revenue has doubled, they are number one in the region for customer retention, and he never received one bad survey for pushing yellows.

The bottom line is, observational coaching is something you can do at any time when presented with an opportunity! Ready to get started? Head on over to my website L2coach.com for a free PDF download of a sample observational coaching form.

Chapter 8

The Fourth Type of Coaching: Turn Around Coaching

The fourth type of coaching is turn around coaching. When trying to come up with a process to help my underperformers exceed expectations, my coach, Keith Rosen, and I came up with Turn Around Coaching. And I was able to develop that into one of my four coaching processes. Turn around coaching is meant to be implemented when you reach the point where you're not sure if an employee is going to make it on your team or not. It's likely they've been with you for a little while, maybe they're not following your sales process, doing the activities they should do, or they're just not putting up the numbers it takes to remain on your team.

Hopefully you see value and potential in them, or you wouldn't have hired them in the first place. And if you did, then what do you owe this person who quit their last job to join your team? A better question might be: what's your responsibility in coaching them up?

Managers in the car business, and many other industries I've coached, usually either hold onto the wrong person far too long or fire the right person way too quickly. It reminds me of my early time in the Army. There was a mural that was in our "chow hall" of a cemetery with the words, "Let no soldier cry out from the grave, if only I had the right training."

A great leader takes responsibility in both the development and success of each individual on their team, is willing to hold them accountable to firm boundaries and expectations, and also takes action to pour into them when they're not. That's what turn around coaching will help you accomplish. You will be able to efficiently identify the right people for your team and separate them from the wrong ones who just aren't a good fit because they didn't rise to the occasion.

One of the things that I realized was that you can't just judge your employee's based on one number or one area. You have to dig deeper and measure them by each area that they would need to be effective. For example, internet lead handling is one skillset. Metrics, walk-in traffic, phones, campaign like referral generation, and service sales are all different skill sets that require different KPIs to measure. So, we separated those things. Suddenly, it changed things. It wasn't, "Oh, he's a bad salesperson or she's a great salesperson" based off their performance anymore. We started realizing everyone's good at something. Very few people are good at everything. And very few people are bad at everything. Most of the time, people have strengths within their realm of job responsibility. So, it became about coaching to people's specific weaknesses while recognizing them for their strengths.

My turn around coaching process is RCP^2. Recruit them to the conversation. Commit to turn around coaching. Party to celebrate they are still on your team. Or Part ways as friends because it didn't work out.

Recruit them to the Conversation

For my dealership, I wanted to give anyone on the cusp of losing their job 30 days to turn around. So, I would meet with them and recruit them to the process. It's just as important that the employee commits to wanting to stay on the team!

A recruitment statement for a turn around coaching convo might sound something like this, "Jordan, what I want for you is that you are able to succeed here and remain on this team long term. How committed are you to remaining on this team?"

You may find out right then and there that the person you're trying to turn around does not want to be there anymore. If so, problem solved.

Commit to Turn Around Coaching

Then, it's important to clarify your intent and share your commitment to them. That might sound something like, "I am committed to helping you remain on this team long term. In order to try and make that happen, we are going to meet up once a week for the next four weeks. We will invest time in helping you meet and exceed the expectations it will take to help you remain on this team. After a month, we will either celebrate that you've made it and you'll be able to stay with us, or it will be apparent you're either unwilling or unable to meet the expectations we coach on. In which case, we will shake hands and part ways as friends."

For the next four weeks, you will meet at scheduled intervals with the under performer, recruit them to each conversation, review which expectations they are not meeting and coach them up! It's critical that at the end of each coaching conversation they are the ones making commitments and executing on those commitments.

As each week goes by, check-in on their progress in between coaching conversations.

Party to Celebrate that They're Still On Your Team! Or Part Ways as Friends

If they aren't changing, growing, and improving, then they've made the decision for you, and it will be apparent by the end of the 30 day period. The dealerships I coach are able to turn around over 80% of underperformers inside of 30 days. About 5% quit during the first turn around coaching meeting during the recruitment convo, and 15% don't commit, follow through, execute, or get the results.

Part ways as friends with those who leave. For those who make it, celebrate that they get to remain on the team! As a leader, it's very rewarding to help people grow in this way, and many will become some of your best employees over time.

With turn around coaching, you can find the perfect balance of accountability with care, where all your employees see how much you value your people, your high level of commitment to them, and that you hold people to the standards it takes to have a winning sales team.

As a manager, I always saw the good in people, and I'd be like 'any day, they're going to turn around, any day,' and then sometimes six months would go by and they still weren't performing and I'd be baffled. There are a lot of times we retain people for too long. We might see potential in them. We might think about the time, effort, and money already spent and not want to see that go to waste, and we hope that they finally get it together. We might also be hesitant to go through the hiring process again and have to train someone else new.

The truth is, keeping someone on the team who just isn't performing is costly for the business and costly for morale. Not only are they wasting time and losing the company sales, but your refusal to fire them is also sending a clear message to the rest of the team. The single biggest reason why holding on to someone too long is a detriment to your company is because low standards are the enemy of commitment and accountability. It's that simple. So when you keep someone on your team too long, and you're allowing those standards to be low, and they're not meeting your expectations, and they're not paying the bills, which sets a precedent for everyone on your team.

The other tendency is to hire someone quickly and then fire them quickly. This is also bad for morale and is a waste of your recruitment investment. It also kills consistency which is important for your customers who want to see the same faces when they come back.

Firing someone too quickly can cause fear in your team. I, like many managers, used to think that wasn't a bad thing. There's this attitude of "at least they'll know I mean business." I and my fellow managers thought it would raise the bar and motivate the others.

However, I've come to realize that this thinking was flawed. Here's what you need to understand: the detriment of this approach is that it pushes people away through fear. When you create a negative outcome or instill fear in your team members, you end up driving them away instead of fostering a positive and productive environment.

It's important to understand that people don't necessarily move in the desired direction out of fear. While their behavior may change, it doesn't guarantee that they will align with your expectations. When we fire employees too quickly, we inadvertently devalue them in their own minds. This fear and anxiety often leads them to start looking for new job opportunities. Although you may initially see temporary improvements, such as increased productivity and calls, these effects are short-lived.

Moreover, as soon as they face challenges or experience a downturn, that fear resurfaces, and they worry about ending up like the previous person who was fired. In these circumstances, employees may feel compelled to prioritize their own financial stability and seek alternative employment. This hasty approach to firing can result in a loss of valuable employees over time.

When I learned about turn around coaching and began to implement it, everything changed. It helped me establish clear expectations for improving underperforming individuals or processes. By providing clear guidelines, you ensure that employees don't have to make assumptions or create their own standards. By implementing turnaround coaching, you can build a sense of value among your employees. They will feel appreciated, knowing that you genuinely care about their growth and success while maintaining high standards for everyone. Ultimately, it's about establishing accountability within your team.

Employees who are underperforming actually crave accountability. Nobody enjoys being in a state of underperformance, and I haven't come across many people, if any, who enjoy going to work

Chapter 8: The Fourth Type of Coaching: Turn Around Coaching

without making enough money. Therefore, it's crucial for you to establish accountability in order to identify individuals who are eager for growth and development, as well as those who may not be the right fit for your team.

Turnaround coaching will assist you in this regard. It will enable you to differentiate between those who embrace accountability and those who do not. This process will also help you determine who is on board with your goals and who may not align with the team's vision.

I had a dealership in Tennessee that implemented the turn around coaching process. They had three underperformers who did not meet the minimum acceptable performance for units sold. All three individuals were put into the turnaround coaching process. One person immediately realized it wasn't the right fit and chose to leave. Another individual, who had initially shown enthusiasm and dedication, struggled to meet expectations and action items after three weeks. Ultimately, they decided to part ways amicably. However, the third person experienced significant improvement and now performs as one of the top phone closers at the dealership.

The team's feedback has been overwhelmingly positive. They describe themselves as the dream team, with increased confidence and a sense of value. The perception of simply hiring anyone with a pulse has diminished, and the cultural challenge of quick turnover has been addressed. The team recognizes the managers' commitment to set standards and invest in their growth. The employees understand that the choice to remain or leave is ultimately theirs to make.

Detach from the Outcome

A crucial piece of the puzzle for coaches and managers when it comes to coaching in general, and especially turn around coaching, is to detach themselves emotionally from the outcome. When we attach ourselves to specific outcomes, we tend to make exceptions and render all our efforts futile. It's crucial to detach from both the positive and negative possibilities concerning our employees. Instead, focus on the facts and the plans you have in place. By removing emotional attachment, the situation becomes clearer and more objective. It boils down to a straightforward assessment: either individuals want to work in their current job role, or they don't. Either individuals are meeting the expectations, or they are not. This mindset shift has greatly helped me.

I always emphasize to managers that it's not about right or wrong when determining the fit of individuals within the team. It's simply about acknowledging the reality of the situation. The question then becomes: how do we discern this reality? How do we identify those who may have said yes to being on the team but might not be the best fit?

Ultimately, after providing employees with a clear plan, support, and training, it's important to be honest with them. If everyone meets the expectations and the provided support and it works well for them, that's fantastic. However, if everyone meets the expectations, but it doesn't align with their needs or abilities, that's okay, too. It's simply a reflection of the reality of your business and the time you can dedicate to them. In essence, if things don't work out, it's not a matter of right or wrong, but rather an acceptance of the reality of the situation.

One individual I tried to recruit into the process for turn around coaching outright expressed their dislike for the job, stating that they hated selling cars and were considering pursuing a different career. Despite liking me and the team, they found the nature of the job vastly different from their expectations. Their interest level rated only around a four on a scale of one to ten. I inquired if there was anything that could make it a ten for them, but they confirmed that it wasn't about me or any changes I could make. Selling cars simply didn't align with their preferences, and they had even anticipated being fired two months earlier. I didn't have to let this employee go myself. They ultimately made the decision to quit right there at the beginning of the turnaround coaching process. It served as a reminder not to become overly attached to the outcome. Had I been obsessed with "saving this employee," there could have been a lot of time and energy wasted trying to save them. Not to mention the frustration that comes with trying to fit a square peg into a round hole!

Chapter 9

Coaching around Limiting Beliefs

Limiting beliefs are indicative of closed minds. In the current automotive retail landscape, rapid change is inevitable. Open mindedness is critical when considering new technologies and processes that can lead to greater success. No manager enjoys dealing with limiting beliefs, and I've coached hundreds of automotive leaders across the country! Limiting beliefs are frustrating for managers because they feel like their employees are making excuses, being lazy, or don't want to grow.

What is a Limiting Belief?

My coach Keith Rosen defined a limiting belief as a SCAM: a Story, Con, Assumption, or Mindset, that is holding someone's success back. Basically, it's a mental roadblock. It's almost always something that is not true, but just perceived to be true. This belief keeps someone from acting to their fullest potential or doing things they're supposed to be doing.

Here are a few real-world examples of limiting beliefs that, as a dealership manager, I was able to address and overcome through coaching:

- Winston the sales consultant – Wouldn't send videos because he thought he looked dumb on video.

- Gary the sales consultant – Wouldn't T.O. (Turn over unsold customers to a sales manager) because the managers were always too "busy".
- Bill the general manager – Assumed his service advisors were lazy and would become frustrated because they wouldn't follow up with their service customers with open R.O.'s (repair orders).
- Roger the Business Development Rep - Believed his internet closing was low because he got "bad leads".

Let's examine each and determine how it's a limiting belief.

- Winston is telling himself a *story*, based on his own imagination and perception. He didn't have any customers telling him he looked dumb.
- Gary is *conning* himself and his managers into believing that he actually tried to turn customers over. Also, because managers always look "busy," he is using that to avoid the T.O. when in fact the managers would almost always prioritize a showroom customer leaving without purchase as top priority.
- Bill's assumption of laziness came from a few bad customer experience surveys. Bill didn't realize that his service advisors were flooded with calls due to a massive recall combined with their third-party call center shutting down simultaneously. The advisor team was already putting in more hours and truly did not have the time to field all the inbound calls and maintain proper follow up with existing customers.

- Roger had a poor *mindset* about internet leads, and this poor mindset came from poor results which came from a poor approach to lead handling. In reality, with proper follow up, he could close around 15%.

Why Do Limiting Beliefs Exist?

In order to coach around limiting beliefs, you must understand why they exist. Activities lead to results, and our brains decide in an instant if the result is a good result or a bad result. If good, our brains reward us with certain hormones like serotonin. If we get bad results, our brains punish us with stress hormones like cortisol. After that, we try to duplicate the results our brains decide are good, and avoid the negative results our brains have decided are bad. The fear of negative output causes people to avoid the behaviors or actions their brains have linked to the negative output.

From our experiences, we are always seeking cause and effect relationships, and when we're not certain that a specific cause created a result, our brains will try to fill in the gaps. These gap fillers are known as assumptions. In short, limiting beliefs are formed from both our rewarded experiences, negative feelings about situations, our fears, and our assumptions about our world.

The Four Mistakes You Must Avoid When Dealing With Limiting Beliefs

Here is what NOT to do, when an employee shares a limiting belief. This is critical because in any interaction with an employee, you are either BUILDING or ERODING the relationship and employee. Here are some of the ways we erode an employee when addressing limiting beliefs.

Don't Go on the Attack

The first thing to avoid is going on the attack. When you go on the attack, you are pushing against their beliefs, and when you push against someone, it's their natural reaction to push back. Push back often leads to frustration, escalation, and conflict. At the end of the day, none of those help the person overcome their limiting beliefs.

Don't Become Sarcastic or Passive Aggressive

It's crucial to avoid becoming sarcastic or passive aggressive. Passive aggressiveness is indirect, and, as such, the employee doesn't have a chance to learn what they need to change.

In addition, this type of demeanor lowers an employee's confidence and saps their motivation. It doesn't end there, though. Ultimately, sarcasm negatively affects the morale of your entire team.

Don't Coerce the Employee

Employees, and especially sales professionals, know when they're being "sold". Asking closing questions to coerce the employee into saying what you want to hear is using your position of authority poorly. Managers who do this often feel like, "My employees just 'yes' me to death, but don't change!" This is frustrating for both parties, and this approach prevents collaboration and, as a result, managers can't get to the root cause of issues. If you don't get to the root cause of issues, then how can you truly solve them? Not to mention, the employee leaves the conversation feeling frustrated saying, "My manager doesn't understand what it's like, nor do they want to." This erodes the relationship and trust.

Don't Ignore the Limiting Belief

Don't ignore the limiting belief of your employee. This is the easy way out, and it's not uncommon for a manager to take the path of least resistance. That being said, think of a limiting belief like a weed growing in your lawn. The longer you let it take root, the deeper the roots go and the harder they are to eliminate. Let too many weeds grow in the lawn, and the entire lawn dies. By ignoring limiting beliefs, you will allow them to further solidify.

It's time to get introspective. When you have an employee with a limiting belief, which of those three unfavorable ways do you find yourself most often reacting? What is your plan to change this going forward?

Tactics for Coaching Around Limiting Beliefs

Now that you know what a limiting belief is, why they exist, and how NOT to address them, it's time to learn HOW to coach around them.

Step 1: Care and Recruit

This should be starting to sound familiar at this point! Instead of attacking, you must care and recruit. Just remember, you can't win a war with a one person army. In the first five seconds of any conversation, people pick a side. Either they fight alongside you to achieve a common objective, or they go on the defensive and fight against you.

Here's how to build a recruitment statement. First, ask yourself this question, "What's in it for THEM if they change this limiting belief?" If the answer is something like, "Increase chance of promotion" or "Increase in sales and profit," then that's your recruitment statement. Simply add, "What I want for you..." to the front of one of those positive outcomes. Finally, add "Is now a good time to discuss that?" after it.

When you put it all together it sounds like this: "What I want for you is to have the best chance for getting promoted. Is now a good time to have a convo about that?"

Step 2: Seek to Understand Their Perspective

Instead of sarcasm, ask open ended questions and seek to understand their perspective. You can't solve an issue if you don't know why it exists. It's the same here. You can't remove a limiting belief if you don't know how it arrived. Some sample questions you could ask are:

1. Where is that belief coming from?
2. What got in the way of you doing that?
3. What outcome did you get when you tried?
4. How did you do it?
5. What was your approach?
6. What else have you tried?
7. How long did you do it for?
8. How does that make you feel?

Don't be afraid to keep asking questions. It's important to drill down to the heart of the matter.

Step 3: Give them Something to Replace the Limiting Belief

Instead of ignoring it, help eliminate their assumptions and give them a new story to replace their limiting belief. Then ask action-oriented questions and commit to driving change. One of my favorite sayings in coaching is, "If they build it, they own it. If they own it, they act on it." Your goal is that they come up with an action plan that will give them the opportunity to let go of the limiting belief and form a new empowering belief that helps them and the business succeed.

Here are some sample questions:

1. What changes do you need to make to get a better outcome next time?
2. What else can you try?
3. Walk me through that approach.

Step 4: Commit to the Plan

Finally, commit to the plan. Remember, your employees will only ever be as committed as you are. This means you need to schedule a check in, follow up from this coaching conversation, and support them as they adapt to change. When people make a change or try something new, they often run into the pain and failure that comes with growth! This is when they're most susceptible to revert back to their old ways. It's critical that you as their leader support them as they transition into their new approach and mindset in order to eliminate their limiting beliefs.

Ask them:

1. When should I check in on your plan to see how it's working out?
2. How do you want me to hold you responsible to your commitments?
3. What can I do to support you around this plan?

Get Rid of Unrealistic Self-Expectation

In addition to our limiting beliefs, there is something else that holds us back and keeps us from being and doing our best. In fact, it's a severe epidemic that is plaguing the business world. As I coach sales leaders throughout the automotive vertical across the country, I uncover this sinister and will-sapping plague time and time again. In fact, due to the frequency of this challenge, I've named this mindset U.S.E. which stands for Unrealistic Self-Expectation. I define

Chapter 9: Coaching around Limiting Beliefs

U.S.E. as when you hold yourself to standards that are impossible to meet or are out of your control. As a result, you become drained, frustrated, unmotivated, and unfulfilled when you hold yourself to standards that you wouldn't hold an employee to, your family to, or even your kids to!

When U.S.E. is uncovered, I ask the person I am coaching, "What is this mindset costing you?"

Client's list unfulfillment at work, demotivation, unhappy life at home, anxiety, lower confidence, lack of focus, activity paralysis, and even depression. What's worse is that while someone is laboring under U.S.E. and has made the mistake of holding themselves accountable to things out of their control, they can't hold themselves accountable to the things they can control. As such, they won't take the right action, at the right time, in the right way that it takes to maximize their results.

Below is a coaching conversation transcript where I was able to shed light on this plague and help coach someone toward a cure. Before you read that, I want to share a traumatic war story that caused me to plummet into the abyss of U.S.E. and share how this damaging mindset reared its ugly head in my career, in the worst possible way. Overcoming these challenging, uncomfortable experiences, while unpleasant, has helped me to coach professionals around this challenge in the business world.

Mosul, Iraq, 2003. Our three-vehicle convoy of HUMVEEs roared down a dusty Iraqi road heading toward the city where our PSYOP headquarters was located in Mosul. My three-person special operations team would travel this route through the sweltering Syrian desert weekly to meet with our commander and First Sergeant.

The trip was always bittersweet. The sweet part was because we were excited for the opportunity to receive our mail and enjoy a slight change of scenery compared to our sweltering, fly-infested desert home to the south. On the other hand, the trip was bitter because the road was often littered with ambushes and improvised explosive devices.

I was the assistant team chief and turret gunner for my team, and I took my job seriously. From my vantage point in the turret, I would remain hypervigilant for the two-hour drive north. Continually scanning the road ahead for debris that could be hiding a roadside bomb which would be set to detonate, destroy, maim and kill as our non-up armored HUMVEE passed. On top of that, as each Iraqi car crept up behind our slow-moving convoy to pass us, I would switch the safety off of my M249-SAW.

The SAW was my thirty-pound belt-fed machine gun I would mount to my turret each time we would leave the wire, which could fire up to eight hundred rounds per minute toward an enemy. As each car passed, I anxiously peered into their windows. The hypervigilance was partly because each car could be packed with a team of Mujahideen fighters. They would carry AK-47 fully automatic rifles ready to unload on us or rocket-propelled grenades that were devastating. Our vinyl doors were no match for any of these munitions and, as such, I wanted to be ready to act in a split second. Regardless of the threat, I decided that I wasn't going to lose someone on my team. I decided I wasn't going to lose anyone on our side for that matter. Unfortunately, while my decision was a noble one, with high intention, it was also a U.S.E. decision and God had other plans.

Chapter 9: Coaching around Limiting Beliefs

As we rolled down a straight stretch of road, the searing hot wind whipping against my face, I noticed something in the deep ditch to the passenger side of the road. Consequently, thinking there was a potential ambush, I quickly rotated my turret and trained the sights of my machine gun on the potential target. As the object crested the drop off on the edge of the road and into my line of sight, I quickly realized it wasn't an ambush.

Instead, it was a tire and wheel well of an upturned civilian vehicle. A few seconds later, I noticed another vehicle in the ditch nearby. The crashed vehicles were white Land Rovers. These were the standard vehicle civilian contractors like the Army Core of Engineers drove. I yelled down the turret over the noisy diesel engine and extreme road noise caused by the aggressive HUMVEE tires to my driver, Specialist Beckman, and told him to pull off to the side of the road.

"Park near the vehicles but stay out of IED blast radius. Make sure we have a clear escape route ahead and watch out for buried explosives or wires!" I shouted.

As we parked just off of the shoulder, our team chief Sgt Rutherford ordered 360-degree security from the rest of the convoy while we investigated the upturned and wrecked civilian vehicles.

What I saw while approaching the vehicles was unforgettable, and for these purposes, I won't go into detail. Know that inside the crashed vehicles, there were a group of ambushed civilians from coalition force countries. It appeared to me that Iraqi Mujahideen forces had pulled up alongside them and unloaded several AK47 magazines into the driver's window and door. Consequently, almost all of them were murdered before the SUV even landed in the ditch.

These allies were Army Core of Engineers who had been carrying explosives which would be used to detonate Iraqi ordinance and for the demolition of unsafe structures. The enemy had decided to ambush them and take the powerful C4 explosives to create roadside bombs. "That could have been us. How could someone take a life over something like this?" I remember thinking.

We frantically checked for survivors and found one. He had a faint pulse and was hardly breathing, but he was alive. We didn't have a medic with us, but we did have a "combat lifesaver". Me. I had gone to the three-day course in preparation for the deployment. There I had learned to give an I.V., splint broken bones, and place a tourniquet on wounded limbs. My driver radioed for a medivac helicopter, which would likely take fifteen minutes to arrive at our location. All the while, I wanted to try and help this save this man from an untimely death with my feeble medic skills.

Due to the lack of confidence in my ability, not knowing where even to start, fearing I would do more harm than good, and having no idea how long they had been in that ditch, I was reluctant to even help. Together, my team and I pulled security and tried to help any way we could. Because of those circumstances, when the helicopter arrived to lift him off, I prayed that the men who had already died didn't have families at home. I prayed that the wounded lone survivor we found would make it through the night. Finally, I prayed I could forget what I had seen because I knew if I didn't forget, I wouldn't be the same again.

Later that day, we arrived at HQ, and, in true military fashion, we had reporting to do around the incident. As if this detailed re-

Chapter 9: Coaching around Limiting Beliefs

count of the experience wasn't enough to reinforce the traumatic experience, a man with tear-soaked bags under his eyes and a British accent approached me and asked, "Are you the one who found my team?"

I said, "Yes, sir." solemnly.

"Thank you…" He paused, trying to hold back tears, his voice beginning to crack. "None of them survived. Their families are going to be devastated." He grabbed my arm and began to cry. "You tried to save them, thank you."

All I could say was, "I'm so sorry."

None of my prayers had been answered, and there was no consoling him. Moreover, I had nothing good to say and no positive thoughts running through my head. All I could think was, "Sean, you failed. You should have been there sooner. You should have done something else. You should have done something more. You didn't practice your combat lifesaver skills. His family is destroyed. You failed your objective to keep everyone safe."

These unrealistic self-expectations or U.S.E. thoughts continued for years. This mindset was so hard to shake it subsequently permeated into other areas of my life like business and family in the civilian world. It took me a long time to realize that this horrific encounter that I wouldn't wish on my worst enemy had rewired my brain to blame myself for things that were out of my control. I began holding myself accountable for events I didn't cause and had no control over.

Fast forward to St. Louis, MO, January 2012. Jeff Cash froze to death while walking home from a local tavern. Alcoholism had claimed his life, God rest his soul. It was excruciating because Jeff was like a brother to me. There were many reasons he and I were like brothers to each other. First, Jeff helped me get hired at the dealership I was now managing. He also helped me get on my feet by encouraging me to keep trying during my first rocky months selling cars. I appreciated the way Jeff would give me training after each customer interaction.

Throughout the next 8 years, he taught me everything he knew about the car business. On top of that, Jeff trusted me to sell to his client base and ensured I always had fresh lists of prospects to call. Moreover, he helped me earn a promotion into finance and then was a massive advocate of moving me into a sales management role.

I had met Jeff about ten years earlier in the finance office when I had just gotten out of the Army. I was purchasing a car to replace the one I had just totaled on my way to work at Best Buy. During my transition from soldier to civilian, I was struggling financially. Partly, the struggle existed because the government had been providing my housing and food. Partly because my mother, who had been taking care of my finances during my two years of combat zone deployments, had also been taking care of my bills. As a result, I became dependent on others taking care of business for me. To make matters worse, I had bought a house I couldn't afford during the subprime mortgage crisis on an A.R.M. loan, and I knocked up my fiancée. Oops!

That's why it was depressing when Jeff announced his divorce, worse when the heavy drinking became evident, and he began his long and steady decline. Jeff drank so much at times that he would pass out at work, and we would have to wake him up by pouring cold water on his head. The most challenging thing I ever had to do as a manager was to fire him. One of the many powerful lessons I

Chapter 9: Coaching around Limiting Beliefs

had learned in the Army was that you couldn't put everyone's lives at risk over one person's self-interest. In this case, Jeff's lack of performance and his inability to function at work was costing everyone steady paychecks and it wasn't fair for the team. I let it go far too long and even had two salespeople quit because they couldn't work with Jeff in his capacity at that time. Regardless, once I finally mustered the courage to hold my friend, my automotive teacher, my career advocate accountable, he completely understood my stance. He thanked me, hugged me, and after he stumbled out of the finance office and I went to clean the remaining items from his office, I found dozens of empty vodka bottles.

As I bagged up the bottles, I thought to myself, "Sean, you failed. You should have seen this sooner. You should have done something else. You should have done something more. His family is destroyed. You failed your mission to keep everyone safe." It was like I was reliving the loss I had experienced in Iraq ten years earlier.

Shortly after that, fearing Jeff was going to drink himself to death, Doug and I tried to help him. Doug was Jeff's best friend and my first manager in the car business. Doug was also the manager I replaced when he quit our dealership about two years prior. We decided to go over to Jeff's house to have a small intervention. When we arrived at his once lively house, I had memories of having dinner with Jeff and his wife. I remembered the sound of his two beautiful daughters laughing and playing, talking about Sponge Bob and chasing me around the house with Jeff's seldom used golf clubs.

Now, it looked like a condemned forsaken house, and upon looking in the window, we saw Jeff sprawled out on the living room floor next to the couch where we used to play Tony Hawks Pro

Skater on his PlayStation. My heart raced, thinking he could be dead. Doug and I were able to get in through the unlocked front door and rushed to Jeff's side. What we saw caused a massive mix of emotions. It was appalling to see that Jeff had fallen on the floor and lay motionless surrounded by his unfinished French fries. Had something terrible happened? Was Jeff dead? Our dread intensified as soon as we noticed no less than fifteen empty two-gallon plastic jugs of vodka strewn across the floor, tables, and counters around his home. Finally, we felt relief to know that Jeff was alive and breathing!

Doug and I were feeling somewhat helpless to prevent Jeff from doing any further harm to himself. Thus, we decided to call the police and ask that they lock him up for his safety. Unfortunately, they couldn't do anything because he wasn't a threat to himself or others. We left multiple messages for AA groups, but it was evening, and they were all closed. We ended up telling the police that our dear friend was suicidal because that allowed him to be locked up for twenty-four hours. As you already know, it didn't save him.

The reason I share this story is that after Jeff died, the same self-defeating U.S.E. thoughts flooded my head. "Sean, you failed. You should have been there sooner. You should have done something else. You should have done something more. His family is destroyed. You failed in your mission to keep everyone safe." Again, I was reliving the loss I had experienced in Iraq ten years earlier.

You see, I had contracted the damaging mindset of unrealistic self-expectational thought. My brain had been wired by what had happened in my past. The first mistake I was making yet again were the demands on myself that weren't fair or realistic. The next error

Chapter 9: Coaching around Limiting Beliefs

was the belief that I could control all of these outcomes and situations. Again, I was telling myself, "No one can be killed on my watch."

These expectations were fallacies, and I was setting myself up for failure. I didn't have control over Jeff's choices or his mental health. Heck, I could barely influence his behavior and had zero influence on the outcome. When you set expectations for yourself that you have no control over, that's utterly unfair to you!

Moreover, when things don't go your way, you blame yourself. As a result, we become jaded, unconfident, fearful, regretful, anxious, disengaged, or negative. We avoid new experiences which could potentially generate the same adverse outcomes. Giving yourself unrealistic expectations becomes a habit, and we begin to punish ourselves repeatedly. We should never hold ourselves accountable to circumstances that we can't influence or change.

This phenomenon occurs in war, and, more frequently, in business. It is the equivalent of working for a manager who continually berates you and punishes you for something like lousy weather, or their favorite sports team losing a game. Except you are the boss, and you are treating yourself like a crap! Does this sound fair to you? Does this sound familiar to you? This challenged mindset must be brought to the surface and addressed post haste. Because our brains operate in thinking patterns, each time you give yourself U.S.E., you perpetuate the cycle when you choose to allow yourself to set the wrong self-expectations.

What happens when you shift your mindset? How can you set realistic expectations for yourself? For what actions and behaviors should you hold yourself accountable? What does it feel like when you free yourself of these atrocious mindsets? What new actions will you take and what can it mean for you in business and sales?

For me to let go of U.S.E., I needed to permit myself to be human. I had to forgive myself for undesired outcomes in which I was involved but didn't have control over. I needed to let go of the outcome and focus on the process and only be accountable for that. I don't have superpowers, and I'm not perfect. I can't predict the future, nor do I have mind control over others. Once I realized these adverse outcomes were choices made by others, and I had given them a life raft to grab onto if they wanted it, I was able to look at things more objectively. Once I realized I would never hold others to these same ridiculous standards to which I was holding myself, I was able to let go. Now, I make much better decisions around what I am responsible for, and, as such, the actions I take are ultimately producing better results.

What I want for you in reading this is to let go and begin to make great choices around what you do have control over. I want you to recognize that when you do have a negative outcome, if you took the right action at the right time and focused on the process and it still didn't work out, that's all you can do, and you need to forgive yourself. Unless you have a crystal ball and can predict the future, this may happen regardless of your process, and that's okay as well. Learn any lessons you can, adjust your process, and continue to take action around what you have control over. Give yourself expectations that you can meet. As such, you can set goals that you can accomplish and enjoy your work and life even more!

Now, let's apply this solution to your business. It doesn't matter if you're a company owner, a manager or a salesperson, cure yourself

Chapter 9: Coaching around Limiting Beliefs

of U.S.E. to improve your skills, take the right actions, and grow as a leader! Here is a walkthrough of a recent coaching conversation where a sales professional I coach was suffering from U.S.E. starting with the last part of our discussion.

"What would make this conversation positively impactful for your career?" I thoughtfully asked. The coaching conversation had started with his greatest challenge.

"I need to get the enjoyment back in my career," he stated.

"Will you tell me more about that?" I asked.

This time he replied with much greater detail, "I'm anxious. I wake up in the middle of the night worrying about my sales. I just want to succeed, and ever since I changed companies, I haven't been as successful as I was before. It's wearing on me, and now when I deal with customers who aren't buyers, I get so frustrated. I left my last job because of these same problems, and I really like it here and want to stay. I'm not sure what to do, I'm just not happy with what I'm doing. I've thought that I might need a career change." I could hear the frustration in his voice.

"Thank you for sharing your struggles with me." I was grateful for his willingness to be vulnerable because this deep level of understanding is where I can add the most value as a coach. "I want to ensure we address anything standing in the way of your career fulfillment in this conversation. Are you open to unpacking each of these challenges separately, then collaborating around an action plan to improve your situation?" These topics were deep, and I needed to know if he wanted me to be a shoulder to lean on for his problems or preferred to address these with actionable items through coaching. I believe without action, coaching is just therapy.

With hesitation and pessimism in his voice, he replied, "That would be great, but I don't think it's possible, and even if it were, addressing this might not be a good idea."

"What would be a bad idea about helping you find less stress, more enjoyment, and success in your career?" I probed.

"Yes…" His initial confidence began to waver. "Well, maybe not." He paused, "I guess the problem is…" he paused again. "I think there are two versions of me. One version of me is stressed out all the time and sells a lot. The other version of me is laid back and isn't as successful."

After coaching many executives, high achieving middle managers, and top producing salespeople who enjoy low overwhelm and excellent results, I knew he was conning himself. I needed to coach him around this con. "Is it possible for someone to enjoy success without high levels of stress?" I probed.

"I think so, and I just have no clue how." He humbly laughed at his own opportunity to grow.

"How successful will you feel about this career if you quit under these circumstances?" I asked another cost-based question aiming to learn if quitting would be an undesired outcome for him.

He quickly and confidently responded, "I would never want to quit under these circumstances because I already did that once at my last job. Also, I like this company far too much to feel good about doing that again." Before I could respond he added, "That's a good point if I don't address this, it doesn't matter if the stress helps me sell more or not, I'll quit again."

I asked him again, "Are you ready to unpack the challenges you've brought up and tackle each one in a vacuum?"

Chapter 9: Coaching around Limiting Beliefs

"Without a doubt!" he said excitedly.

"Other than success, stress caused by your inability to unplug from work, and unruly buyers, what other challenges should we address here?" I wanted to ensure we had clarity on where to begin.

"That's pretty much it. If we can tackle those, I think I can get to the level of success I want here," he verified.

Since words like success mean something different for everyone, I needed him to paint that picture. "First, I need to understand what success means to you. Can you help me understand what that looks like?"

He quickly threw out a result, "I would sell twenty cars a month and make about ten thousand dollars."

"In addition to the units and commission, what about that level of success is so important to you?" I asked.

"Matt, who recruited me, needs me to knock it out of the park. He told me that when he hired me, and I promised him I would do it. I just want to make him happy. Also, I don't want to go back now that I've already been to a certain point of success at my old dealership." He clearly felt like he was letting Matt, his hiring manager, and himself down.

"I respect you for wanting to please your new manager and exceed his expectations. How far off his expectations are you?" I questioned him further.

Silence.

"How many cars does *he* want you to sell, and what does he expect you to make each month?" I asked another way.

Chuckling softly, he said, "I don't know. He's never really given me a specific number."

"What is causing you to feel that you're not meeting your manager's expectations? Has he given you any sign that you're underperforming?" I wanted to know if there were non-verbal cues such as body language, or passive-aggressive behaviors coming from his manager that may indicate frustration.

"No, not at all." He paused.

I asked, "What assumptions might you be making about your manager's expectations of you?"

"All of them. I need to talk to the boss and find out, don't I?"

"Sounds like a great idea!" I allowed my enthusiasm regarding his idea to show. Now it was time to turn an idea into an action item or plan, "Are you willing to do that?"

"Absolutely. I'll do it right away," he declared.

As I took notes around his first commitment, I asked a follow-up question about his past performance, "Also, in your prime, how many cars were you selling at your old dealership?"

"My last full year at my old store, I sold about two hundred and fifty-five cars!" he proclaimed proudly.

I wanted to find out how far he had declined since joining this new team, "Now, how many cars per month are you selling?"

"I've been here for about four months. I had a rough first month, we were really slow, and I sold about thirteen. I told the dealership it was my fault for hiring me." He laughed. "My second month was amazing, and I sold twenty-seven cars! The last couple of months have been pretty good. Selling about twenty." He finished there.

I jotted "U.S.E.?" in my notebook regarding the way he was potentially blaming himself for the dealership's lousy month, and I also began to do the math on his results. Next, I asked, "Okay, other than the company you work for, and your results, what else has changed?"

Silence.

"Have you been doing everything the right way? As in, are you following your processes, working as hard as you usually do, and being personally accountable?" I dug deeper.

"Well, it took me a while to get used to the new pricing system here. It's been such a cultural change from my old company. I had to learn a whole new way of doing business. I feel like I've got it down now, though," he stated.

"Okay, great, thank you!" I said excitedly. I was excited because I now had the information I needed. I believed I had uncovered the puzzle pieces he was missing. The missing puzzle pieces were the ones I had, and that's where I can make an impact. I had to verify this before I attempted to add value, but there was still the matter of the customer frustration. "I think we are arriving at a point that I can help you with your greatest challenge. Before we do, what is it that you enjoy and dislike about your customer interactions as it relates to your career responsibilities?"

"I really like educating them, training and bettering people. When they are open to that sort of thing." I could hear the passion in his voice again. Then the spark faded as he explained the downside in detail, "Nowadays it seems customers always know what they want. They have done their homework and don't want to deal with a salesperson anymore. It's like they want to get in, get the best price, and get out. Some of them are only concerned about price and come across as downright rude. I don't think it's fair to be treated like that when they don't even know me."

I replied with another question, "What does a rude customer sound like?"

"They don't want help, won't let me ask them questions to help them, or teach them anything."

"It sounds like you have already identified your ideal customer. Someone who wants to learn, gain an education, and enjoys a two-way dialogue. Is that correct?"

"Absolutely," he stated.

"Also, it sounds to me like you have defined your brand in the automotive sales world. Something like #TheAutoEducator I help people learn about and find the perfect car for their families!" I was ensuring we are aligned in his definition of his personal brand.

"Ok, this is almost creepy! At my last dealership, they used to call me the Car Professor!" He laughed.

"Have you chosen to use this brand to find, attract, and engage with customers to set expectations with and create your ideal customers?" I asked.

"I can't say that I have."

It was time for me to drop the coaching hammer and give him the missing puzzle pieces. Most professionals have 97% of what it takes to achieve what they want most in their head. It's the 3% of puzzle pieces they don't have, that as a coach I need to uncover. In that way, each piece of information I share, every story I tell, is a guaranteed value add. "It's time for me to add value… are you ready to grow as a person and a professional?" I confidently asked him.

"Please!" he said.

Chapter 9: Coaching around Limiting Beliefs

"First off, what would it mean for you if you could wait on customers who wanted to work with someone like you each and every time?" I asked, seeking to crystallize this new possibility further.

"It would mean the world to me," he said hopefully.

"What I want for you is that you enjoy working with each customer that you choose to work with because they like buying cars from a knowledgeable salesperson such as yourself. I want the customers you work with to seek out and appreciate the level at which you educate your customers."

I was recruiting him to the conversation because people choose a side within the first ten seconds of a conversation. I wanted to be candid, and this can cause people to become defensive. To ensure he knew the positive intent I wanted him to choose the side that would fight for him, his coach's side.

I stated bluntly, "Then choose to wait on those customers, and choose to walk away from the rest. Give the customers who wouldn't be enjoyable to work with to someone else. If you were going to enact a process to screen customers and allow yourself to wait on customers that would positively impact your attitude and actions, what would that look like?"

"I would tell them how I sell cars upfront, the automotive educator, then ask them questions to see if they would want to work with me, and vice versa. I like the idea of defining my brand and process upfront. Maybe I could even talk to Matt about letting me learn service," he replied.

"Sounds like a great plan," I said.

Wanting to tackle the U.S.E. problem, I asked the following question, "Regarding your success levels... If you were my manager, would you ever get angry with me, browbeat me, think less of me, and treat me like a second-rate citizen for not meeting expectations that you never gave me?"

"Of course not."

"Is it possible to sell perfectly and still not make a sale?" I asked.

"Yes," he replied.

"Why?" I asked.

"Because you can't control all the customer's decisions, no matter how good you are in sales. No one can get everyone to buy," he wisely answered.

Time to drive the point home and show him that his success hadn't backslid near as much as he believed it had. "Now imagine you are my manager, and I was learning an entirely new process. I am your employee following that brand-new process and working my tail off. During that learning phase, I sold about 1.2 fewer cars per month. Would you be angry with me, browbeat me, think less of me, and treat me like a second-rate citizen for taking that much of a dip in results?"

"No, I wouldn't. Not at all."

"Then WHY are you doing THAT to yourself?" I asked.

He was quiet.

I raised my voice for maximum impact and memory retention, "Is there any value in browbeating yourself for results you have no control over if you are following the right process? Is anxiety, fear, and the result of quitting worth the payout of slightly better performance in the short term? Is it fair for you to think less of yourself and believe your manager feels you aren't meeting expectations when you don't even know what expectations you're not meeting?"

"No, to all that," he replied.

In reality, you're selling two cars less per month than you were before, while learning all this new stuff at a new dealership, and each month you're selling more! That's impressive!" I wanted him to start winning immediately.

"Thank you," he said with gratitude.

"Are you willing to commit to waiting on more of the right customers, and create more of them knowing there are so many customers out there who would kill to work with a salesperson like you?" It was time to finalize his action plan.

"Yes. One hundred percent!"

"What mindsets and behaviors are going to be different from here on out, and what is your action plan after this conversation?"

With a chuckle and sigh of relief, he said, "I am a dick of a boss to myself… First off, that's going to stop." The relief came as his mindset had shifted to a higher level of thinking, and his long-standing pent-up anxiety finally began to fade. "Looking back at my results, I'm happy with how I've done since the job change. I think I can do even more for my company when working with the right type of customers, or even in the right department. I think this conversation has ensured I'll be with my company longer and can't wait to sit down with Matt, find out if he is happy with me or not, and discuss all this." He wrapped up with his action plan, "I am going to focus on what I can do and not stress out about the outcome. I'm going to tell my customers how I sell cars up front!"

As a result of our coaching conversation, He was now ready to hold himself accountable to activities that were in his control, instead of results that he could barely influence. Equally important, he was ready and willing to meet with his manager to clarify his leader's expectations in a dialogue instead of assuming he was failing to meet them. He gave himself credit for learning so much and not going backward as terribly as he had perceived after looking at factual data. Finally, this fantastic individual committed to begin selling in a way that aligned to his core values and beliefs. Doing so has ensured he creates more career fulfillment and avoids the feeling of hopelessness created when your environment, people around you, and behaviors aren't moving you toward what you want most in your career and in life. Remember, U.S.E. is useless.

What's Holding Us Back?

The only thing getting in the way of what someone wants to accomplish is what they "think" is getting in the way. After having thousands of effective coaching conversations where a clear objective is defined, any limiting beliefs holding the client back are coached through, and the coachee commits to a plan in order to accomplish what they want, I can safely say something pretty profound.

98% of the barriers holding you back are COMPLETELY SELF IMPOSED.

This is profound because if 98% of the obstacles that are holding you back are self-imposed, that means 98% of the time you have it within your power to achieve what you want!

Earlier this week, I relished a coaching conversation with a dealership executive. The following dialogue is a detailed outline of the

Chapter 9: Coaching around Limiting Beliefs

conversation and the perceived barrier to success that was absolutely crushed with one single coaching conversation.

"We just aren't able to get where we want to go." The frustrated operations director named Joe claimed.

Joe was an extremely talented 62-year-old man with a proven track record. Successfully managing dealerships for decades, he had won the prestigious silver pin award from VW, only a tiny fraction of Volkswagen leaders earn this. In addition to talent and success, Joe had a ton of motivation. He was driven by the fact that he was retiring in four years. The thought of retiring didn't excite him. What did get him fired up was leaving a legacy of success and knowledge.

The dealership owner, Mark, was a second-generation dealer, about fifty years of age. Mark has a son named Tim, a 30-year-old manager and potential future dealership owner. Joe was excited to join the organization because he wanted to mentor the owner's son in order to leave the car business and Mark's dealer group better off than he had found it.

"What's getting in your way, Joe?" I asked.

Joe replied, "There isn't one thing… In fact, there are a lot of things. First there's Tim. I told him three months ago that we need to get our used car department in order. We were going to get back together and create reporting to identify our ideal inventory. After that we were going to create a plan to start getting rid of aged inventory. Well, he never came back to me with his plan. Now it's been three months, we have a ton of inequity in our inventory because all the cars have depreciated, and he keeps buying cars making things worse. There's no discipline!" He paused.

"What else is getting in your way?" I asked again to further peel the onion.

Joe sighed, "Another issue is Mark. He's supposed to be the owner of the dealership, yet he walks through the showroom floor and sees something he doesn't like. Right away he grabs the employee, pulls them aside and starts in on them. He does it in a way that makes the employee feel attacked and more often than not, I would find out about it and address it anyhow."

I could tell he had more to unload, but in my head I wondered why that bothered him. My assumption was that everyone would want the owner helping to observe and coach their team. I held onto my assumption and patiently asked, "What about that is so frustrating to you?"

"Well, it lowers the morale of the team, and it creates a situation where when I address it later it creates a "the beatings will continue" sort of situation. Also, it undermines the authority I have, and when Mark gets angry at the people on the team, they think that I am failing as a leader. Due to the history of high turnover in my position, this makes people think I might get fired," he stated solemnly.

I could tell Joe was troubled by this situation, and I could empathize. At this point, we had been coaching together for about six months. During my cultural assessment phase at this dealership, many employees shared their past experiences with managers in Joe's role. The owner would interview people for this role, hire them, get angry with them quickly when expectations were not met, and fire them after only a few months. I wanted to bring some positivity to the conversation, "That's nothing we can't overcome in this conversation! What else is bothering you?"

Chapter 9: Coaching around Limiting Beliefs

"Okay, well the GSM Brent has been here forever, and he's kind of bought in, but kind of not bought in. I think that if him and his assistant were to really get behind Mark's vision that we could take this store to another level. It's like he does just enough to get by, but he's not all in. And then there's Carl the finance manager, don't even get me started on him. He resists and argues with everything we do all the time, but he generates so much revenue for our dealership…" he paused a moment before continuing again. "It's as if there is constant undermining of Mark's initiatives and constant destruction of our game plans, and everyone just waits for things to change again because we don't follow through."

Respecting his willingness to take ownership, I asked him, "I hear you saying the word 'we.' What role are you responsible for playing here?"

He thought about my question for a moment and replied, "It's my role to hold people accountable to these things and make sure they get done."

"Sounds easy enough!" I joked to lighten the mood.

He chuckled slightly amused and replied, "It would be if this were me at my old dealership. I used to run this VW store, and I had this team around me that didn't accept mediocrity and always wanted to grow the business."

"I'm curious. Back then if your managers at your old dealership were behaving like this, how would you have handled it?" I asked, believing that inaction wasn't a choice he normally makes.

"I likely would have fired anyone who didn't get on board," he replied without hesitation.

I was a little shocked by his brash response from a leader I know values employee retention. In fact, when he first hired me to be his coach, one of his goals had been to eliminate turnover. In the six months of working together, we had already almost completely eliminated turnover. I was also curious as to his reasoning for doing the exact opposite now, so I asked, "Just like that? Tell me more."

"Well, I would try to train them, give them my expectations, and try to improve their buy-in and performance first," he claimed, realizing he came across a little harsh.

To uncover the significance of this I warmly asked, "What would it mean for you if we could accomplish that here?"

There was a long enough pause that I thought our call dropped and just as I went to check my phone he replied, "It would mean everything. But you know what else, the owner at my old dealership was different. He told me exactly what he wanted me to do, how to do it, and what I was responsible for. He told me if I did those things he would be happy. So I did them, and he was happy. I don't know what Mark wants. I mean we've lost money the last 5 years, and I've been here almost a year, and we're going to net over one million dollars. But he's still not happy, and I don't get it."

"What's different now?" I questioned.

Sternly Joe replied, "Mark is too involved, and the team here has been here for years and they're like family to him, and I don't know what he wants." He paused again then asked, "What am I supposed to do, write his son up for not following through? End up firing him or something?"

Chapter 9: Coaching around Limiting Beliefs

I decided to take the bait. It was time to help educate him by helping him come up with some answers, "There are three challenges that need to be addressed here. The first is regarding your need for clear expectations from Mark. How can you win the game if you don't know the rules?" I asked.

"I can't," Joe replied.

"Let's assume you can get that clarity. How would you do it?" I asked.

"I would ask him to clearly define his vision for next year. What do you want to achieve? I would make sure it's real specific." Joe was already starting to sound hopeful.

"That sounds like a great idea," I replied while jotting that down as a potential action item. I say potential because he hadn't committed to it yet.

I asked another question, "The second issue to resolve is that the managers are not getting behind the growth you and Mark want. What could be the worst possible outcome if you hold them accountable and responsible in the way you know you need to?"

A thoughtful reply, "I get fired for trying to make them better."

"And how would you feel about that outcome?" I asked.

"I would be disappointed that I chose to spend my last years before retirement at the wrong place. A place I thought I could leave behind better than I found it. It would mean that they didn't really want to grow. So, I guess if it came out in the wash like that, I'd be okay with being fired," he said calmly.

People often focus on the worst-case scenario negative outcome. In order to help him consider positive possibilities I asked, "Knowing Mark's frustration with the managers' execution, what could be the most positive possible outcome if you held them responsible and accountable?" I asked.

"It's more likely, knowing Mark's frustration with the managers, that they'll probably do what they need to do in order to remain on the team, and then everyone wins. Mark will trust that I can get the job done, the managers get better, and we achieve even more growth," he stated with confidence.

"And if you continue to do nothing and take a back seat?" I inquired.

"We won't grow, may go backwards in results, or worse I'll end up getting canned or quitting out of frustration," Joe said.

"How many of these barriers are self-imposed?" I asked, hoping he was realizing the same thing I was.

"You're right, all of them!" he proclaimed.

It was time for Joe to commit to action, "You ARE empowered. You CAN do what needs to be done. What ARE you going to do? Give me your step-by-step plan!" I demanded excitedly. This conversation had me pumped up.

Joe confidently replied, "Before this month is over, I am going to sit down with Mark and get his vision for success. Then I am going to demand excellence from the managers, and if they don't rise to the occasion, I will hold them responsible. Every one of them will be required to step up, even Mark's son, or I will move them into a different role and find someone who can and will do it."

Not a bad plan, but I saw an opportunity for him to get even better results when gaining clarity that would take him past one year. It was time to add value and co-create, so I recruited again before asking a question, "Joe, I want for you to get the clarity you need to

Chapter 9: Coaching around Limiting Beliefs

carry your career success all the way through to retirement. Are you open to exploring some ways to accomplish that in this plan?"

He nodded, "Yes, please."

"What's the difference between a goal you want to achieve and a vision for success?" I questioned to verify the missing puzzle piece.

"I guess a goal is more short term, and a vision is something bigger and over a longer period of time," he replied.

"Exactly! So how far will a one-year goal take you, as opposed to a five-year vision for success?" I smiled awkwardly knowing that my question just gave him the answer. I jotted down a note to reflect on later and grow as a coach—try avoiding questions that give people the answer. It's selling! Even master coaches still make mistakes.

He laughed, "You're right. We need a longer vision for success and many annual goals tied to them! That way, we know what we're working on long term, and I won't have to go back to the well every year to figure out what his expectations are."

"What changes will you make to your plan?" I asked.

"I'm going to get his long-term vision for success, five years out, instead of going for a year," he replied firmly.

To ensure proper care for the plan I asked, "What can I do to support you and your team around this?"

"It would mean a lot to me if during your next visit, you facilitate a vision meeting for us. You've got a lot of experience in that, and I think it would be important to have our coach involved. Would you be willing to help with that?"

"I'm in. Let's do this!" I replied with a smile and enthusiasm.

As the coaching conversation wrapped up, Joe and I had a newfound respect for each other. Together as a leadership team we clarified the vision for success which included creating the best customer experience, loyal employees and customers, strengthening the leadership bench, creating problem solving sales and service leaders throughout the entire dealership, and even dealer group expansion adding a truck lot and another manufacturer. Over the next couple years, the dealership achieved many of those goals toward making that vision a reality, including purchasing a Dodge Ram truck store in their market!

Chapter 10

Measuring Success through Coaching

There's a saying that what gets measured gets done. What we're doing with coaching is trying to implement long-term behavioral change. We have to be able to measure that.

Many times, managers find themselves repeatedly expressing the same ideas in hopes of achieving a different outcome. Despite their efforts, the desired results often elude them, leading to frustration. I am here to assist you in breaking this cycle, eliminating redundancy, and fostering the replication of successful endeavors.

Occasionally, individuals achieve remarkable feats without a clear understanding of how or why they were able to do so. These instances can occur by chance, even when circumstances seem to work against us.

My objective is to empower you to identify the triumphs that stem from coaching interactions. By achieving this, you can guide employees in duplicating these victories and extend their replication throughout your organizational workforce.

You can create measurable success through coaching. In order to do so you must first create a coaching culture. Then you must learn to track coaching consistency. Finally, you must learn to create a coaching win while duplicating its success.

Creating a Coaching Culture

Creating a coaching culture will help you accomplish the positive long term behavioral change it takes to maximize your success in any kind of market. You will be able to eliminate redundancy in your leadership routine which will allow your management team to be more efficient and effective with their time. This will help you duplicate and re-create success throughout your department, while helping you gauge the effectiveness of your coaching.

You've been given most of the tools to accomplish this, now it's time to learn how to put them into practice!

Learning to coach will change your life, creating an entire coaching culture will change the lives and success of your entire company. As you're learning from this book, the benefits to a coaching culture are vast, and for you managers taking that step with the intent to grow as a leader, I am truly excited for you and your people.

In order to create a coaching culture, there are a few steps that must be taken. You can follow my acronym D.R.I.P. to make it happen.

D - Discover

D stands for discover. The first part is discovering what everyone on the team wants to accomplish in the long term, and individually setting goals with each person. If there's anyone else on your team for whom you still need to learn their vision for success, set goals, and find out their expectations around how they want to be coached, now is the time!

Chapter 10: Measuring Success through Coaching

Providing someone with a form and instructing them to complete it is a somewhat impersonal approach. While this method allows you to review their responses, a more impactful strategy involves engaging in deeper conversations. After the initial form-filling, you can sit down with them again and encourage them to elaborate on their answers.

When you take the time to pose thoughtful questions and actively seek clarity while maintaining an insatiable curiosity, your coaching efforts become significantly more effective. This approach not only demonstrates genuine care but also fosters a stronger connection. Granted, when dealing with a considerable number of individuals, such an approach might consume a substantial amount of time. Nonetheless, it's important to remember that coaching demands both curiosity and patience.

Curiosity is not a mere checkbox to be marked off before moving on to the next task. I challenge you to engage in genuine, meaningful conversations with your team members. These interactions will remain etched in your memory. For instance, when you gaze into someone's eyes and inquire about their career aspirations in the next six months, and they earnestly express their desires, the exchange becomes memorable. You delve further by asking them why these aspirations matter so much to them. This type of dialogue leaves a lasting impression. Reference back to chapter 4 on setting your GPS if you need to revisit how to do this.

Also, it's important as the leader of your team that you clarify your vision for success. What do you want to accomplish most, and how could each individual fit into your vision? The value of a clarified leadership vision was outlined in the coaching conversation with Joe and his dealership owner at the end of the last chapter.

R – Recruit

R means recruit. You're going to need to get "buy-in" with the team, including all of your managers, around coaching. When I decided to create a coaching culture at my dealership, I sent out a team email memo letting them know what we were doing, and why we were doing it. Also, I communicated what was in it for them if they participated in this new culture. At the time, I believed a coaching culture was going to change the game for us, so I let the team know how critical this was going to be for our success as a company moving forward, and theirs as individuals. Why is creating a coaching culture going to ensure short-term and long-term success for you, your team, and your business? What will be the reward for those who fully participate? What will be the likely consequence for those who avoid the growth? Answer those questions thoroughly and thoughtfully, and ensure you communicate your reasons to everyone.

I – Individually Set and Learn Expectations Around Coaching

I stands for individually set and learn expectations around coaching. Remember, coaching is more for the coachee than the company or the person doing the coaching. To that point, it's critical that a two-way expectation sharing conversation occurs. This way, the employee will know how the manager plans on coaching: types of coaching, frequency, duration, etc. Additionally, the manager giving the coaching can learn how to tailor the coaching for each person they will be developing in this way.

P - Persist

P means persist in making it a habit. Coaching convos can happen anytime, anywhere. That being said, intentional scheduling will ensure you are making the impact you want and need to have for your team, and that no balls are being dropped. You're going to create a coaching cadence and calendar. You'll get the tools for that in chapter 12.

Track Coaching Consistency

Tracking your coaching activity is key to having effective coaching because it creates accountability and consistency around the coaching efforts, and gives the coach and coachee the notes they need to ensure each session builds on the last. With all these coaching conversations taking place each month, there are a lot of moving parts. That's why it's KEY that you are using some sort of system to document and track your coaching efforts with each individual. Additionally, these type of documented coaching efforts can be valuable in lowering legal exposure from disgruntled employees whom you must terminate or who quit for other reasons.

Tracking Systems

It doesn't matter what system you want to use. If you're old school, a file cabinet with hanging folders and notebook paper can work. Though we are in the 2020's and, as such, you may want to consider something in the cloud like Microsoft OneNote, Google Drive Docs, or something along those lines.

If you were to hire my company to coach with your team, we provide these tools for you, but as of now, you may need to build your own system for documenting and tracking coaching.

First, create a coaching file. The manager giving coaching is responsible for maintaining this file. Name the file something like this: Sean Kelley (or you can use your name instead of mine, hah) Coaching Team 1 2023.

Next create a separate sub folder for each employee who will be receiving coaching: Joe Smith Coaching 2023.

Six Things to Document

There are six specific items you will want to document for each employee. It's important to know what those are and how you will use the documentation later.

1. **Their GPS and long-term vision for success.** This way you always have something to coach on! With their GPS, you will be able to reference this and continue to accomplish existing

goals, and set new goals, until their vision for success becomes a reality. And when that happens, create a new 3-to-5-year vision for success by doing a new GPS!

2. **Their expectations around coaching.** You want these documented so that, as a coach, you can circle back and ensure you're meeting them by tailoring your coaching for the individual.

3. **Each tactical coaching topic.** By documenting the topic of each coaching convo, you'll get in the habit of zeroing in on a specific topic, avoid having the same convos with the same people, and be able to reference the individual's growth over time.

4. **Employee action plans from each conversation should be documented.** In this way, you can ensure their commitments are written down for accountability and follow up later.

5. **The manager's coaching commitments.** Remember, your employees will only ever be as committed to their plans as you are as their leader. That's why your action items to care for the plan should also be documented.

6. **Coaching wins.** Documenting any time, a new behavior, attitude, or improved result comes from a coaching convo will help you as a leader know who's getting the most out of your

coaching sessions and reinforce the impact of this behavior for you and the person you're coaching.

Create Coaching Wins and Duplicate Success

The ultimate goal is to create coaching wins and duplicate success. In chapter 4, we discussed the learning process outlined by Abraham Maslow whereby someone goes from unconsciously incompetent, to consciously incompetent, to consciously competent to unconsciously competent where they've mastered the skills to the point where they don't even have to think about it.

Let's talk for a moment about the second stage, consciously incompetent, where someone realizes they know what they can't do. This is where the toddler is learning to walk. This is where the kid is learning to tie their shoes. This is where the manager is learning the leadership language of coaching. It's *not* going to go perfect the first try, or maybe even the 2nd.

It's critical we give ourselves and others permission to learn something new. We must give ourselves and the people we coach the grace, care, support, and accountability it takes to succeed as we all learn and grow. That's what caring for the plan will accomplish in the short term and long term. It will ensure the action plans from the coaching conversations lead to positive long-term change.

In this way, a coaching convo and the care for the plan is a lot like the front end and back end of a car deal. Imagine the initial coaching conversation is like the sales floor, and the care for the plan is like the finance office. You need both for a profitable deal. Often, when people try something new, adopt a new mindset, or try to get new results they're going to struggle. When they do it's easiest for them to default back to the old way of doing something. This is where you as their leader come in with care, accountability, and support to help them through their change. Just know that failure when trying something new isn't the *exception* to the rule of growth, it's the *expectation*. Don't browbeat your people, no differently than you wouldn't torment a toddler who falls over when learning to walk.

This is why we've documented the coaching topic and the action plans and are checking in on them after each coaching convo, either before the next session, or at the beginning of the next coaching conversation. When checking in on the last plan, one of two situations has occurred: it worked, they changed and already got better results or they're still struggling.

If it worked, congratulations! You created a coaching win. Immediately, you want to use the 4-step recognition process that we touched on earlier to duplicate and perpetuate the behavior:

- Step 1. Acknowledge the specific behavior or area the coachee improved.
- Step 2. Let them know how their change will positively impact the team.
- Step 3. Let them know what's in it for them if they continue the desired behaviors.
- Step 4. Ask them to continue the behavior.

All four steps are important. The first one recognizes that they accomplished a goal. It's important to do so, but in order to encourage continued change on a behavioral level you need to take it farther than that. You need to show them how that change positively impacted the team, underscoring that in order to continue to positively impact the team they can't consider this just a one-time accomplishment that they can check off on some list. Finally, you need to let them know how it will continue to be good for them if they continue in the improvement or change. This is how you implement long-term change.

On the other hand, let's say you touch base and they either haven't executed on their plan, or they've tried and aren't getting the desired results. It's time to coach them through it! Recruit them to the conversation, ask some great coaching questions to uncover what went wrong, discover any limiting beliefs getting in their way, and ensure they re-commit to their action plan!

- What's getting in the way of you using what we coached on?
- How did you try it?
- What did your approach sound like?
- How did your customer react?
- How many times have you tried it?
- If accomplishing (insert goal) is still important to you, how will you do it if you don't make these changes?
- What else can you try?
- When will you recommit to starting, or trying this again?
- How can I support you as you continue to make this change?
- What do you want me to do in order to hold you accountable for your plan?

Chapter 10: Measuring Success through Coaching

One of the biggest gaps in leadership, and this is for any business, not just the car business, is misaligned expectations. The leader wants someone to do X, Y, and Z, and expects it to be done a certain way and expects specific results. The employee often doesn't have line of sight to that, isn't even aware of that, and that's really not fair to them. So, the purpose of coaching, one of the ways that I define effective coaching, is that the coach and the coachee have aligned with their expectations.

Both people need to know what's supposed to happen, what they're supposed to do, and be okay with that. It's as simple as, "I like your game plan. I like the expected results. We're on the same page. Let's shake hands and make it happen." So, once you've aligned those expectations and both people know what the result is supposed to look like, and what actions it's going to take in order for that result to occur, everyone's on the same page.

Coaching is about helping people move closer to their objectives, even if it's just an inch of progress in a single day. Each small coaching win accumulates to achieve ultimate victory, akin to winning a war through the accumulation of countless battles. There is no magic solution or silver bullet in coaching; instead, it involves engaging in conversations that clarify goals, challenge limiting beliefs, drive behavioral change, and produce measurable actions and outcomes.

Chapter 11

Inspired Satisfaction

Coaching meets a lot of motivation requirements and can help in retaining employees by helping them achieve a high level of inspiration from their leaderships' business culture and a strong sense of satisfaction in their work. As it relates to leadership, I believe there are 4 C's you need to be aware of. The first three being: Caring, Competence, and Character. When a manager invests time in their employees in coaching, it shows care. When the manager has the organizational skills, discipline, and focus to follow through with the care needed to support each employee around the initial coaching conversations, it raises the leader's competence level in the eyes of all parties involved. When the manager supports the individuals through barriers that inevitably arise when trying new things, learning a new skill, or adopting a new behavior, it raises the leader's character level in the eyes of all parties involved. This type of leadership is one of the contributing factors that causes employees to choose to work for a manager and remain on your team each day. This is why I believe Coaching is the 4th C of leadership.

Inspired Satisfaction: How to Get More Motivation from Everyone and Predict Employee Turnover

Every employee has a chance of turning over. They could outright quit their job, be recruited elsewhere, or you could terminate them. While the probability is there and many external factors outside of a manager's control could affect an employee's likelihood of quitting, the majority of actions that can directly lower this likelihood are under the leader's control.

Green Pea Profit Loss: For this topic, the term "Green Pea" means new to your dealership. After measuring turnaround metrics from dozens of dealerships CRM's, the average new hire takes close to 40% more "Ups" or opportunities than their more seasoned counterparts. Regardless of waiting on more customers, they often close at 35% less than an employee who has been there for over 6 months. If your veterans are waiting on 30 customers and closing at 60%, it's safe to say your new hires are waiting on 45 and closing at 30%. When an employee understands your process, customer, product, the team, etc., after working somewhere for at least 6 months, they will close significantly more deals per month versus their greener counterpart.

Impact on the Rest of the Team

"They'll hire anyone with a pulse" is the red flag that flies high when I interview sales teams. Bringing in new employees can often cause stress on the rest of the team and create indicators like that one, which imply your business has reached an extreme amount of turnover. Your team has broken, and people may refuse to help the new hires, and rather they become just a number. Instead of wanting to get to know, work with, and help the new hire, this will create a mindset of "They won't last here anyway."

It's at this point that managers are all alone in the quest to recruit, hire, train, and coach new salespeople. The rest of the team will begin to hinder your efforts. Standards drop to a new low for new hires and veterans will no longer believe they are a part of something great. This lowers employee motivation, and high producers on your team have leverage because they know that they will be harder to replace. Hopefully, they won't use that against you.

Impact on Customer Retention

Customers feel the turnover, too, especially the customers who would stay loyal to your dealership and bring repeat business and referrals. When they come back in and see a new employee who doesn't understand them or get to know them, all the rapport and relationship that initially made the deal is out the door. Astute customers may even wonder, "Why are there always new salespeople in this place every time I visit?" They want to go somewhere where everybody knows their name. The implication of high employee churn is extremely costly to your company and has a further reaching impact than most managers give it credit.

Predict the Future

There is a surefire method for understanding the likelihood an employee will leave or be terminated. Looking at the illustration, there are two Axis.

The X-axis determines the level of employee motivation. There are several key factors involved. First is the number of the 10-employee motivation requirements that are being met and to what capacity. Of the ten needs, managers usually meet only two or three that are most important to them in their own career. If an employee has different primary needs, they often feel neglected by management. As a result, employee morale can slide left on the axis, showing a lower morale which ultimately creates a less than desirable employment situation.

The Y-axis determines the level at which their livelihood needs and wants are being met in relation to their perception of being able to have them met elsewhere. In addition, it involves the employee's success as perceived by their managers. The reason these two factors must be combined for this measurement is because if an employee is meeting their criteria of success at a job, but their manager doesn't believe so, they are likely to be engaged differently by their manager.

Chapter 11: Inspired Satisfaction

On the other side, if they don't feel successful at their job, or aren't meeting their personal expectations of success, but the manager feels they are, they will be treated as such. This ultimately raises their perception of success on the Y-axis. Both internal and external factors may influence where an employee lands on the Y-axis.

Perception is the key word here because perception is reality. An employee may feel they are as successful as they can be in their role at their current place of employment, but do they feel they could get closer to their version of success elsewhere? If they do, they will slide down on the Y-axis and the likelihood of their staying at your dealership decreases immensely. The quadrant that they fall into will determine the likelihood that they will quit, be recruited, be terminated, or stay as long-term employees.

The top right corner: this is Inspired Satisfaction. The employee's engagement needs are being exceeded. The employee believes that they are more successful than they would be at any other place of employment. Their manager perceives them as successful and a top producer for the company. The employee's overall morale is high. This employee will remain a happy engaged employee for a long time to come.

The top left corner: this creates Driven Success. The employee feels successful at their job and their managers feel that they are successful. The employee believes that they are doing the same or better at their current place of employment than they could do elsewhere. However, there are engagement needs that are not being met. As a result, the employee's morale is lower than it could be. If they are in the Driven Success column, the employee may have a low likelihood of quitting because they are meeting their personal expectations of paying their bills and career success. However, these employees are susceptible to recruitment from other companies. All it takes is for them to believe that they could be more successful or equally successful elsewhere. A close network or a potential new manager can convince this employee that the work conditions and motivation requirements will be better elsewhere. If this happens, they are likely to move on to greener pastures on the morale side.

The bottom right corner: I call this Lackadaisical Fulfillment. These employees are your friends, they are treated with respect, and have high morale levels. However, their personal version of success is not being met. It is perceived by others, and often their managers, that "they could do more". Frequently, these employees stick around because they enjoy the people that they work with or enjoy the job or place of business in and of itself. These people may be challenging to fire because a manager has built a positive relationship with them. However, these people are susceptible to being removed from the company because they do not meet expectations. They may also quit of their own volition because they are not able to live up to their own career success standards. There is a fairly high probability that a company with high accountability, goal setting, and standards for achievement will terminate this employee.

The bottom left corner: this final quadrant is Frustrated Disengagement. This is when employees are disengaged because motivation requirements are not being met. Their career satisfaction is low and they often believe that they can do better elsewhere. These employees are more than likely already searching for external opportunities. They often take bold, negative action against the company when removed from the organization or willingly departing. The employees in this category are the ones most likely to file suit, make a formal complaint, or damage your organization's brand when leaving.

Keeping them on without doing anything is a grave mistake as they may be disengaged and could cause damage as an employee. They won't look out for the company because they don't believe the company or manager is looking out for them. They need to be coached quickly into another quadrant to avoid damage being done to the manager's reputation, the dealership's brand, and the overall health of the organization. Their likelihood of being employed at your place of business without action being taken is slim to none. Plan on replacing these employees within 30 days.

A manager's return on investment (ROI) of time spent with their employees is extremely important to shed some light on. Managers should spend at least one hour per week with an individual employee in order to improve each employee by 10% over the course of 3 months. However, new hires generally take up a fair amount of this time. This causes the middle of the pack employee and top producing veterans to get neglected. 10% improvement of a higher producing employee shows a much higher ROI of managers' time. In perspective, 10% of a 10-car person at $2000 a car will result in 1 more deal and $1100 more profit vs 10% of a 20-car person at $3000 a car resulting in 2 more deals and $6600 more profit. The coaching question becomes, how can you spend this necessary time with your A and B players if you're constantly working with your C players and interviewing to replace those that quit?

We as leaders must upgrade our leadership style, ability, and knowledge just like we upgrade technology at our dealership. We must find new and creative ways to meet employee motivation requirements to ensure that our team members enjoy coming to work. We also need to ensure that we are aligned to each employee's personal expectations of career success and financial satisfaction. In this way, we understand their goals and objectives and can help ensure that they meet them. When we work with our employees, and these goals are not aligned to the company goals, the employee's comfort zone needs to be stretched to reach new heights. Only by doing so can we ensure our employees reach inspired satisfaction and remain loyal to us and our leadership. Building a coaching culture at your dealership will help you accomplish all this and more.

Chapter 12

Creating Your Coaching Cadence

Rhythm is important not to just to music, but also to life. It's particularly crucial when dealing with workflow.

There's a rhythm, a cadence, that you should be bringing to your coaching that will help order and balance out what you have to accomplish and when.

Your coaching cadence will depend on a few factors, not least of which are the types of coaching you're doing, how many managers will become leaders who coach, and how many people are on your team.

One of the objections many managers come up with to spending the proper time and energy coaching their team is that they just don't have enough time.

I know it might seem like as a manager your entire job is running around putting out fires all day, and that just doing what you have to still has you going home long after the business has closed for the evening.

What if I told you that developing your coaching calendar and finding your coaching cadence would actually give you back time and create more order while decreasing your stress levels?

If you've read this far into this book, I'm sure you see why this is possible. But just in case, let me explain how a coaching cadence changes the game.

Coaching Buys Back Your Time

Much of a manager's job is reactive. There are a hundred things a day that are vying for your attention. I think one of the biggest S.C.A.M.'s that I hear is when managers are talking about their barriers to effective coaching.

One of the biggest limiting beliefs is that they just won't find time to coach. I understand. I ran a very busy, high-volume retail business, and before I learned the secrets to effective coaching I spent all day with my hair on fire, trying to solve one problem after the next. I felt like I was always reactive, and I couldn't get ahead of anything.

Coaching changes that whole scenario. I know it's hard to believe that your business can be totally different or your role at the dealership can be proactive. There is light at the end of the tunnel. Coaching is a proactive approach to getting everything done that you need to get done.

Coaching empowers your people to take initiative, it develops their minds to turn them into problem solvers, it transfers the skills necessary that prevent the need to chase lost sales, and it ensures the people unwilling to meet expectations, who are often our biggest time drains, either put up or get out.

Initially, you may doubt the feasibility of conducting so much coaching in a month. However, by the end of this, with the visual coaching cadence calendar, I hope to demonstrate that it is indeed possible and achievable.

Aspirational Coaching

Aspirational coaching focuses on meeting the employee's engagement needs and addressing their career goals. It's about helping individuals advance within the company and achieve their desired outcomes. This approach demonstrates care for their growth and enables them to accomplish what they aspire to, whether it's moving up in the organization or pursuing personal ventures like real estate investment.

Aspirational coaching can also save you time. I had an employee named Vince who expressed his ambition to be groomed for a management role. During our discussions, I discovered that Vince possessed exceptional spreadsheet skills. Recognizing his talent, I integrated his strengths into my management routine. This proved advantageous as I previously spent around two hours daily logging deals on a shared Google Doc. By delegating this task to Vince, who excelled in spreadsheet management, I freed up valuable time and improved efficiency.

By aligning an employee's aspirations with their skills and finding ways to incorporate those skills into existing processes, you not only support their growth but also optimize your own productivity.

The process of logging deals was a source of frustration for me. It involved capturing every rebate, incentive, and chargeback from the sales transactions, including front and back profits. The task was time-consuming and demanding. I would attempt to keep up with it throughout the day but often fell behind, ending up working late into the night, sometimes until 10:30 or even midnight.

As a manager, I often questioned whether there was a more efficient way to handle this responsibility. Then, when discussing Vince's career advancement goals, he offered a solution. He suggested taking over the logging task, relieving me of the burden. However, I hesitated to grant him access to the company sheet, as it contained sensitive data intended for leaders only.

To address this, Vince took the initiative and created a separate Excel spreadsheet. This allowed him to handle the logging process independently. What impressed me was that he integrated a formula into the spreadsheet, which connected it to the CRM system. All he needed to do was input the stock number for each delivered unit, and the spreadsheet automatically populated the necessary information.

Delegating this task to Vince not only saved me valuable time but also ensured that the essential data was accurately recorded. It was a win-win situation, as he was able to showcase his spreadsheet skills while lightening my workload. This example demonstrates the benefits of identifying individuals' strengths and finding efficient ways to delegate tasks, ultimately improving productivity for the entire team.

He was able to accomplish that task in less than 30 minutes a day, and I only needed to spend about 10 minutes reviewing it before logging it. This efficient process saved me nearly two hours every day.

So, you can see that this single coaching conversation, which lasted an hour, had a significant impact on my time management. It allowed me to delegate the right task to the appropriate individual, fostering his growth and motivation. Employee growth, including career advancement, is one of the ten essential requirements for employee motivation mentioned in the "Inspired Satisfaction" chapter.

By leveraging aspirational coaching, I can empower others to take initiative, effectively delegate, and drive extreme motivation. Of course, this approach also minimizes the need for extensive management involvement since coaching involves asking questions that prompt individuals to solve problems themselves.

Observational Coaching

Observational coaching also saves time in the long run. During role-playing exercises and customer interactions, such as proposing deals, we provide support to our employees for improvement. However, it's crucial to consider other steps in the process as well, such as meet and greets, internet lead handling, and needs assessments. While managers often focus on observing the proposal stage, it's essential to broaden our scope of observation.

If we solely observe the proposal stage, it's akin to solely watching a baseball player swing the bat, ignoring the other aspects of the game. In baseball, a team's success depends on more than just hitting home runs. Similarly, we must incorporate observational coaching for all stages of the sales process, including interactions, delivery, and needs assessment.

Observational coaching is vital for saving time since it enhances skills and reduces the need for constant manager involvement around lost sales. When our employees become more proficient at closing deals, handling deliveries, assessing needs, and building value, our customer satisfaction index (CSI) improves. This coaching method minimizes the frustration of micromanagement and allows us to identify and address behavioral issues early on.

Through the "start-stop-continue" model you learned about in the chapter on observational coaching, we can guide employees in determining what behaviors to adopt, eliminate, or maintain. Once a behavior becomes ingrained, it requires less formalized training and more quick check-ins and reinforcement.

To implement observational coaching effectively, I recommend dedicating 30 minutes per employee every other week. Focus on one step in your sales process or one aspect of employee-customer interaction. In the car business, I recommend observational coaching for greetings, assessing needs, walk-arounds, negotiations, inbound phone call handling, or responding to internet leads. By covering two topics per month in these regular check-ins, we can foster continuous improvement and save valuable time in the long run.

To ensure behavioral change, it's important to establish regular check-ins. After coaching on a specific topic, observe the employee's performance the following week and note any changes. Repeat this process with a new topic for a week or two. By observing the same behavior or activity repeatedly, you can assess whether the employee has made any improvements. This approach allows you to cover two coaching topics per month.

To track progress and motivate employees, I recommend utilizing a tool like typeform. This tool can be customized for each dealership we coach. For example, in our Mercedes store we coach in Nashville, we created a scorecard specifically for walk-around presentations. Product concierges, who oversee deliveries and other aspects, use this tool to evaluate salespeople during walk-arounds. Delegating coaching responsibilities to the product concierges has freed up managers' time. The results of these evaluations are automatically emailed to managers, providing valuable insights.

Implementing a scorecard and tracking system is beneficial for monitoring observational coaching. Even if it's a simple printed sheet, clearly define expectations for a walk-around and record scores for each employee. By consistently tracking and documenting observational coaching, you can identify patterns and measure the impact of coaching behaviors on desired outcomes.

Additionally, tracking coaching behaviors and their correlation with results can be significant. For instance, when implementing leadership led weekly phone scorecard coaching at a dealership we coach in St. Louis, Missouri, we experienced a notable increase in phone closing percentages, exceeding 15%. By connecting coaching behaviors to improved outcomes, you can strengthen the case for the importance of observational coaching, and buy back a lot of time.

ABC Metrics Coaching

As the leader, you have the power to identify the data that needs improvement and devise a plan to achieve it. Metric coaching saves time by eliminating processes that are unprofitable or offer little to no value. Let me illustrate this with an example.

In one instance, a store purchased a robust technology tool for their service operations at a cost of $2,000 per month. The training required about 20 hours per month for three consecutive months for all employees involved. Additionally, managers had to allocate an extra 30 minutes to an hour per day to use the new tool. While money was being spent on the tool, it was also consuming valuable time.

To assess the impact of the tool, we implemented metric coaching on a weekly basis. This allowed us to monitor the metrics and determine if the tool was positively affecting the store's results. However, during the coaching process, we discovered that the tool was not integrated with their CRM system, or their dealership accounting DMS system, and was not providing the expected incentives and rebates.

After consistent metric coaching for approximately 45 days (about a month and a half), we realized that the tool was not going to yield the desired outcomes. By canceling the tool, we saved the dealership a significant amount of money and freed up the managers' time. In this case it made sense to return to what had been proven to work effectively. On top of that, the business owner had clarity as to why it wasn't working and supported his managers in this decision and even said, "Without coaching, I would have been mad at my managers and probably even chastised them. Coaching helped me with clarity and, as such, instead of chastising I've supported them."

It's worth noting that trying new tools, processes, and technologies is a worthwhile endeavor as it has the potential to revolutionize operations. However, in this case, we encountered critical technology gaps that rendered the tool ineffective. It's a common scenario where tools end up collecting dust on a shelf, costing us money each month. Metric coaching can prevent such wasteful investments and all the wasted time put toward implementing the wrong ones long term.

For a recommended cadence of metric coaching, I suggest evaluating and reviewing metrics on a regular twice a month basis. Earlier, I shared a story about someone handling internet leads who was the lowest performer, who didn't want them, and thus shouldn't have been taking them at all. This incident occurred approximately seven years ago, highlighting the importance of metric coaching over time. Seven years of having the same wrong person underperform in a key area of opportunity would have cost the business hundreds of thousands of dollars over time.

Metric coaching is a valuable practice that saves both time and money. By closely monitoring and analyzing the metrics, we can identify inefficiencies, ineffective tools, and unprofitable processes. This enables us to make informed decisions, optimize operations, and achieve better results.

I recommend 30 minutes of metric coaching twice per month. So for the sales team, pull up a sales report. Do metric coaching for each individual. Coach to come up with a game plan on that metric. Then factor in the check-in to care for the plan. The back end "check-in" is five minutes per employee every other week, on the weeks you're not metric coaching.

Turn Around Coaching

As you've learned, coaching up an underperformer plays a crucial role in addressing the individuals who consistently fail to meet the business's expectations and needs. These are the employees who make promises but do not follow through, or simply aren't meeting performance expectations. Expectations such as not making the required calls, lack of prospecting efforts, failing to engage with customers as promised, or not meeting minimum results.

However, with effective coaching, it is possible to turn these individuals around and guide them toward meeting the desired standards. This approach can help retain valuable employees and prevent making hasty termination decisions that may prove detrimental in the long run.

Moreover, coaching saves time by addressing the issue at hand rather than investing unnecessary resources in managing underperforming employees. When an incorrect fit exists within the team, it can be likened to a situation in the military where it takes three soldiers to care for an injured soldier in combat. This consumes valuable time and diverts attention from investing in individuals who truly contribute as builders within the organization. By focusing on our top producers and high-performing team members, we optimize our time and maximize productivity, resulting in a gain in overall performance.

I recommend looking at your bottom 10% or even 20% producers in each department and putting them into your turn around coaching process where you would give them 30 days to turn around. You give them one hour per week, and then an additional ten minutes each week checking in to see if they are following through on the action plan.

Empower Your Employees to Think for Themselves

One way you can save a lot of time is by empowering your employees to think for themselves instead of running to you for all the answers. In my B.C. (before coaching) era, prior to transitioning from a manager to a leader who coached, I was the primary problem manager of my business. As such, I found myself constantly reacting to angry customers and closing deals. It became a cycle of stress and feeling overwhelmed. However, one of the most valuable tools I implemented was a powerful autonomy question that significantly increased autonomy within my team and helped them navigate challenges.

One key aspect of coaching is enabling employees to think for themselves. Often, employees become dependent on managers to solve their problems and provide answers. This dependency creates a barrier to scalability and prevents the manager from breaking free from a reactive management style. To overcome this, it is essential to develop a team of problem solvers, and coaching plays a vital role in achieving that.

When employees approach you for assistance, whether it's while closing a deal or scheduling a demonstration with a customer, you can grant what I like to call guided autonomy to empower them by asking a simple question:

"I'm happy to share my thoughts on this, but before I do. You know this customer better than I do, I trust your skills and believe in your ability to solve this. What do you think it will take to accomplish the next steps here?"

This statement and question acknowledge their proximity to the customer and conveys trust in their abilities.

By posing this question, you encourage employees to think critically and make decisions independently. It fosters a sense of ownership and responsibility, empowering them to solve problems and handle situations with confidence. This approach can be applied across various scenarios and interactions, such as desk deals or assisting customers online.

I was visiting a dealer group in New Jersey. Nicole was a competent, direct, and efficient leader who oversaw a large dealership group call center. She had just gotten back from vacation and approached me, saying, "Sean, I had some time to reflect on how I could make my team better."

"What did you come up with?" I asked.

"I spend a lot of time and energy answering everyone's questions. And al lot of them are things they should know."

"What about that bothers you?" I prompted.

"Well, I want them to be able to come to me and I want them to know they can use me to support and help them. So, my fear is that if I start telling them they should know that and shut them down that they won't get the help they need or they'll think I don't want to help or manage them," Nicole explained.

I sought more information. "How do you handle it when they ask you something they should know?"

"I tell them the answer."

"How does that work out for you?" I asked.

"It doesn't. They keep coming back for more answers."

It reminded me of this time a peacock showed up at my house and we started feeding it cat food and it stayed and crapped all over my deck. If you keep feeding something, it will come back for more. People take the path of least resistance. If it's easier to ask their manager, that's what they'll do. And if it doesn't work out, the onus is on the manager so that's even better.

I looked at Nicole and asked her the next question. "If they come to you seeking an answer you think they should already have, what would empowering your people while showing them you want to help sound like?"

She didn't hesitate. "Hey, you've been a part of this team for some time now, you're well-trained, you're knowledgeable, in your opinion what's the answer to that?"

She put the policy of responding that way into play right away. Within a couple short weeks her employees were problem-solving on their own, they were answering each other's questions, and it bought her back time in her day.

Overall, the practice of asking the guided autonomy question promotes a culture of problem-solving and empowers employees to think for themselves. It is a valuable tool that helps managers transition from a reactive approach to a proactive one, enabling them to focus on more strategic initiatives and effectively scale their team.

Once I started doing this, I discovered that about half the time they came up with a better answer than the one I would have given them. It was powerful stuff. And I'd say, "Wow, great idea. Go do that." It really made me realize how smart the people on my team were. It also helped me know who I can really trust because when your employees give you their answer and it's better than what you thought of, then it's amazing!

If the answer they come up with isn't a great one, you can still empower them. This is where the word "guided" in guided autonomy comes in. Say something like, "Let's walk through your solution to that problem together to explore likely outcomes and see how we can improve the approach. What specific result are we aiming for?" and "How does that plan accomplish this result?" It's important to follow up with the question of whether the identified result aligns with their expectations and goals. If they realize that their initial solution won't work, it's time to brainstorm alternative approaches. Encourage them not to fear suggesting ideas, and if their solution doesn't seem viable, it gives you the opportunity to prevent potential negative outcomes by leveraging your experience and insight. This approach is almost like having a crystal ball that allows you to see into the future. How fun is that?!

Here's the intriguing part: When you simply dictate what they should say or do, it's not as effective as when they come up with the solution themselves. By allowing employees to contribute their own ideas, they are more likely to take ownership of the solution and follow through on its implementation. This approach taps into their sense of autonomy and accountability.

Encourage open dialogue, offer guidance when needed, and be attentive to any uncertainties or requests for clarification. This approach fosters a collaborative and empowered work environment.

There was a particular incident where the boss of a customer did not receive new car gas during the delivery. Instead of immediately providing an answer, I asked David, my team member, what he would do in that situation as a manager. Initially, he seemed hesitant, but I insisted on hearing his thoughts.

After a moment of contemplation, David suggested printing a gas slip and asking his boss to sign it off, while also considering adding it to the deal as a goodwill gesture. I was impressed by his response, as I hadn't considered the option of adding it to the deal. I empowered him to proceed with his proposed solution.

This experience of David solving his own problems was a turning point for him. It demonstrated the value of coaching and empowering employees. As a result, I observed a positive shift in my own workload. The time I used to spend dealing with these types of situations, as David and other employees would often pass them on to me, significantly decreased as a result. As a store manager, this saved me about an hour a day.

Witnessing the impact of coaching and empowering employees was truly remarkable. It not only allowed me to focus on closing deals and analyzing metrics, but it also facilitated the time necessary for the growth and development of my team. This experience reinforced the value of coaching, enabling leaders to work efficiently during their scheduled workday as opposed to outside of it. As a leader who coaches, there's much reward in the trust and confidence knowing that your team is capable of executing tasks at a high level. It creates an environment where teams can excel and achieve success while minimizing the need for constant managerial intervention.

Understand the Coaching Capacity Necessary for Your Team

- Aspirational coaching sessions require one 45-minute session per employee per month plus 5 minutes to touch base every other week (10 if there's something to discuss).
- Observational coaching sessions require two 30-minute sessions per employee per month plus 5 minutes to touch base every other week.
- Metric coaching sessions require two 30-minute sessions per employee per month plus 5 minutes on the other weeks caring for the plan.
- Turn around coaching requires four one-hour coaching sessions per person that you've put in the program per month plus ten minutes a week to check in.

If you are the only coach, and have ten employees with two in the turn around coaching program, that comes out to be a total of 36 hours per month. The first coaching cadence calendar in the next section shows this example.

Also keep in mind, one person doesn't have to do all the coaching. Two or more managers can split the coaching load, cover for each other, and maximize everyone's time. In fact, the second calendar shows this type of example with two managers who are revolutionizing their leadership by coaching splitting the team into two. Requiring less than 20 hours of coaching per month, per manager.

For those of you reading this who are still thinking, "There's no way I can spend 36 hours of my time coaching my people," I want to hit you with some hard truths, and a couple questions to get you thinking in the right direction.

A manager wants to jump into the fold and close deals for their employees. A leader who coaches wants to make their people so good that the leader seldom ever needs to jump in. This mindset is the difference between adding additional sales versus the multiplication of sales. It's the difference between falling behind as a manager of a team versus growing your market share as a leader who coaches. If you are indeed a manager, and one of your job responsibilities is in fact to develop the people under you, what percentage of your time should be devoted to doing tactical sales work yourself, and what percentage should be devoted to making your people better so they can all sell more?

If your answer is at least 25% of your time devoted to multiplying your skills and results through the development of your people, then 36 hours of this within a month makes perfect sense.

Build a Coaching Cadence Calendar

Once you know how much of each type of coaching you will be personally handling, you can create a calendar to make it simple. Do things in blocks so that you're focusing on one type of activity and handling several employees back-to-back. Here is the sample coaching cadence calendar with one manager coaching 10 employees. 36 total hours within a month, using the four types of coaching you've learned in this book.

August 2023

Sunday	Monday	Tuesday	Wednesday	Thursday	Friday	Saturday
		1	2	3	4	5
	5 X Metric Coaching Sessions Employees F, G, H, I, J: 9 am -11:30 am		5 x Aspirational Coaching Sessions Employees A, B, C, D, E: 9 - 1 pm	2 x Turn Around Coaching Sessions (As Needed) 1 - 3 pm	5 x Observatrional Coaching Sessions Employees A, B, C, D, E: 1 pm - 3:30 pm	
6	7	8	9	10	11	12
	5 X Metric Coaching Sessions Employees A, B, C, D, E: 9 am -11:30 am			2 x Turn Around Coaching Sessions (As Needed) 1 - 3 pm	5 x Observatrional Coaching Sessions Employees F, G, H, I, J: 1 pm - 3:30 pm	
13	14	15	16	17	18	19
	5 X Metric Coaching Sessions Employees F, G, H, I, J: 9 am -11:30 am		5 x Aspirational Coaching Sessions Employees F, G, H, I, J: 9 - 1 pm	2 x Turn Around Coaching Sessions (As Needed) 1 - 3 pm	5 x Observatrional Coaching Sessions Employees A, B, C, D, E: 1 pm - 3:30 pm	
20	21	22	23	24	25	26
	5 X Metric Coaching Sessions Employees A, B, C, D, E: 9 am -11:30 am			2 x Turn Around Coaching Sessions (As Needed) 1 - 3 pm	5 x Observatrional Coaching Sessions Employees F, G, H, I, J: 1 pm - 3:30 pm	
27	28	29	30			

Here is the sample coaching cadence calendar with two managers coaching 10 employees, effectively splitting the load, and both managers making time to coach each other on Tuesdays.

August 2023

Sunday	Monday	Tuesday	Wednesday	Thursday	Friday	Saturday
		1	2	3	4	5
	Coach A: 6 X Metric Coaching Sessions. Team 1 + F&I: M: 9 am -12 pm	Coach A: Aspirational Coaching Coach B 10 - 11 am	Coach A: 6 x Aspirational Coaching Sessions Team #1 + F&I M 9 - 2 pm	2 x Turn Around Coaching Sessions (As Needed) 1 - 3 pm	Coach A: Team #1 + F&I: M: 6 x Observatrional Coaching Sessions.1 pm - 4 pm	
6	7	8	9	10	11	12
	Coach B: 6 X Metric Coaching Sessions. Team 2 + F&I: N: 9 am -12 pm	Coach B: Aspirational Coaching Coach A 10 - 11 am	Coach A: Observational Coaching Coach B 10 - 11 am	2 x Turn Around Coaching Sessions (As Needed) 1 - 3 pm	Coach B: Team #2 + F&I: M: 6 x Observatrional Coaching Sessions.1 pm - 4 pm	
13	14	15	16	17	18	19
	Coach A: 6 X Metric Coaching Sessions. Team 1 + F&I: M: 9 am - 12 pm	Coach A: Metric Coaching Coach B 10 - 11 am	Coach B: 6 x Aspirational Coaching Sessions Team #2 + F&I N 9 - 2 pm	2 x Turn Around Coaching Sessions (As Needed) 1 - 3 pm	Coach A: Team #1 + F&I: M: 6 x Observatrional Coaching Sessions.1 pm - 4 pm	
20	21	22	23	24	25	26
	Coach B: 6 X Metric Coaching Sessions. Team 2 + F&I: N: 9 - 12 pm	Coach B: Metric Coaching Coach A 10 - 11 am	Coach B: Observational Coaching Coach A 10 - 11 am	2 x Turn Around Coaching Sessions (As Needed) 1 - 3 pm	Coach B: Team #2 + F&I: M: 6 x Observatrional Coaching Sessions.1 pm - 4 pm	
27	28	29	30			

Chapter 13

Onward and Upward

"For God so loved the world, that he gave his only begotten Son, that whosoever believeth in him should not perish, but have everlasting life." – John 3:16

Six months into Operation Iraqi Freedom, we moved from central Iraq to northern Iraq and took refuge at an inoperational oil refinery. We made it our base because it had a fenced-in perimeter, was centrally located to the cities where we would be running our missions, and provided many other strategic advantages. The refinery also had many vacant living spaces where past refinery workers used to live back when it was operational. These made for great soldier living quarters due to their mud brick construction and surprisingly decent amenities like sinks and showers. We called it our "hooch".

One of the issues with the oil refinery was that a few dozen Iraqis still lived there, and we weren't allowed to displace them for various reasons. As a result, living on the refinery required us to have guard duty around each of our living quarters within the guarded perimeter of our compound. The extra guard duty offered protection in case one of the refinery workers happened to be an insurgent or threat. With a three-person special operations team, this was taxing on our availability to sleep.

Shortly after setting up camp at the refinery, we discovered a wild dog lived behind our hooch. It was the scrawniest, mangiest, most torn-up mutt I've seen in my life. As such, we rightfully named him Scabby-Do. At this point, we were absolutely sick of eating the government-issued meals of MREs and began feeding many of the scraps to Scabby-Do. We trained Scabby-Do and played fetch with Scabby-Do for fun. We cared for Scabby-Do. Over the weeks and months, Scabby-Do grew all his fur back, became extremely muscular, and fell in love with my team. For the record, you never get tired of saying Scabby-Do's name!

After a month or so, whenever an Iraqi came near our makeshift home, Scabby-Do would go on the defensive to protect us. He watched over us so well we didn't need to keep guard duty up for our building. Scabby was on top of guard duty 24/7 and would alert us with snarling growls and ravenous barks when any outsider would so much as look at our building.

We were up late on Christmas Eve, celebrating in our hooch, trying to enjoy the holiday in the war zone. Suddenly, Scabby-Do went haywire, barking like we had never heard before, and ran off into the darkness. We grabbed our weapons and got ready for battle. Before we could seek targets outside our mudbrick building window, two high-impact explosions rocked our building. The jolt shook us and our home to the core.

Someone had fired two RPG rocket-propelled grenades at our hooch. Enemy insurgents had broken through the infantry security around the perimeter of the refinery and launched the grenades at us hoping to kill and maim us. Had they had a direct hit, or worst found their mark by hitting our door or window there would have

Chapter 13: Onward and Upward

been casualties and I may not be writing this book. Luckily, both grenades had missed. One missing low, hitting the pavement just in front of our door, and one off to the side of our building. We believe thanks to Scabby-Do's love and vigilance for us, we got to live to fight another day. Scabby-Do came back later that night slightly injured from the insurgents he saved us from with a look on his panting face that said, "Did I do good? Gimme more MREs!"

The story provides a few valuable leadership lessons. Feed your people the knowledge and skills they need to become strong and succeed within your base of operations. Build relationships with them, and they will look out for you. Care for them and love them like family; they will go to war for you. Every leader needs a helping hand from time to time. Be the leader your people need to thrive; they, just like Scabby-Do, will have your back.

I have a passion for helping people and I believe the best leaders do, too. When I coach, I feel like I am fulfilling my life purpose by helping others fulfill theirs while improving and enriching their lives both professionally and personally. It's a wonderful feeling, very spiritual in nature, when you know you've made a difference in someone's life.

In some ways, I didn't realize just how much of an impact I'd made on how many people until I was hospitalized and incapacitated for months and nearly died from COVID-19. The outpouring of love and prayers I received at that point was overwhelming to me. The messages from the amazing people I'm blessed enough to coach during my time in the hospital confirmed I was on the right road, spending my life helping them grow. It also showed me in a very real way how precious and fragile life is and that we shouldn't waste a moment of it being where we aren't supposed to be or doing things that don't fulfill us. I documented my entire journey through the hospitalization and the revelations it brought me in my book *The Visitor: How a Near-Death Covid Experience Taught One Man Faith, Prayer, Love, and Charity Are God's Remedies to Survive and Thrive.*

When you look around at the world, you see people that are dying inside. They're struggling at work, they're struggling at home, and they're scared and uncertain about the future. I see more of that every day and it breaks my heart.

That's why I was no longer content to just run my company and help a handful of individuals and dealerships at a time. I want to help more people. I want to train managers to develop themselves as leaders. I want to multiply the leadership growth by helping leaders change their teams, their families, and the world for the better. This leadership revolution starts with the manager, it starts with you, and it starts with sacrifice. Pouring into your people sacrifices your time and your energy, and you give up your chance to be the hero by making them the heroes. It requires you to change the way you engage with and communicate with those on your team, and that's sacrifice.

One of my favorite verses in the Bible is John 3:16 which speaks to the incredible love and compassion that God had for us. He sacrificed His only son for us. One life for all of ours.

Before that, the law dictated that for every sin there had to be a sacrifice. I can't even imagine how many sacrifices I would have been called upon to make throughout the years for my transgressions big and small. Imagine all that sacrifice, all that death when multiplied by millions of people? It's astounding and tragic.

Then imagine all the people in the world and just one sacrifice one time for everything. That's transformative. It changes lives. It changes culture. It changes ritual and tradition. It changes everything.

While I was wrapping up this book, John 3:16 started popping up everywhere. It was on street signs, billboards, mentioned by others in random coaching conversations, sent in videos to me on social media, my hotel room number, and more. It was like I couldn't not see it or hear it in some fashion everywhere I went. Being a believer, I became convinced that God was trying to tell me something and the timing wasn't just a coincidence.

I think He is trying to coach me like I coach my clients. I'm always pushing them to think bigger, dream bigger, set the next goal. I think that's what He's telling me now. I think.

I've been working on writing this book for over five years, so it's a goal that's finally been accomplished. I wanted to reach more people than I was reaching through my current business platform. I think God's challenging me to think even bigger, beyond managers in car dealerships to managers and leaders in all businesses and all walks of life. He's challenging me to follow Him and do what I can to change the leadership culture in this country and, eventually, the world.

Coaching changes everything. It takes the failing employee and turns them into a superstar. It takes the average employee and turns them into a money-making machine who donates to cancer research. It takes a great employee and turns them into the employer who then creates a business of great employees who eventually might become employers as well.

Can one book change the world? We know for a fact that it can. I've been trusting God that this book would change the world for at least a few people, but I know He's asking me to step out in faith and grow that vision into something more. When I figure out exactly what that looks like, I'll let you know.

But now I have a question for you.

What more is God calling you to do? What is the dream that you've had that's seemed out of reach or not worth telling others about or just plain impossible? It's not. Find yourself a good coach and talk to them about what it is that you want in the short-term and the long-term. Reach out to me, I'd love to help. At the very least, reread this book and use it to start looking inward.

This book was written with the intent to help anyone reading it to revolutionize the way they lead their team by learning the leadership language of coaching. I'd like you to take some time now and reflect on how you can also help yourself.

Set your G.P.S. Figure out what your purpose and its significance is by answering the questions in the GPS in chapter 4. Then start setting goals for yourself. Once you know what you want and why you want it, it will be easier to achieve.

Go through some aspirational coaching on yourself using the DRIVEC3 method.

Discover what you want in the future and what you want now.

Recruit yourself to the conversation.

Inquire to build the puzzle, find out what it is that you've been missing.

Verify that you've found your missing puzzle piece and add value.

Chapter 13: Onward and Upward

Educate yourself and challenge yourself to come up with solutions.

Create an action plan and commit to it.

Confirm the value of the coaching.

Care for the plan long-term.

Now, some of those will be very hard to do without your own coach, but you can at least get started in several of these areas while you're acquiring one! For metric coaching and observational coaching (the second and third types of coaching), you're really going to need someone to help you through those as you work on your goals. The fourth type of coaching, turn around coaching, hopefully won't be necessary if you've been honest with yourself about your purpose and your reasons for it, and you've set goals that are in alignment with them and your core values!

If you find yourself hesitant to start on your own action plan, goal achievements or encounter roadblocks, you'll need to take a look at your limiting beliefs. We all have them. These are the things that almost always aren't true but are lies we've bought into or bad mindsets and habits that we're clinging to. Once you blast those limiting beliefs with the truth, then you should find moving forward on your goals to be significantly easier.

Example: Some managers have the limiting belief that if they make their people too good, they'll quit and go elsewhere or even that their business owners will replace them as a manager with the successful up and comer.

Truth: Employees who are better, make more money, and employees who make more money are less likely to quit. Moreover, owners never fire leaders who turn the individuals on their teams into superstars.

Make sure you set benchmarks so that you can measure success. You need to be able to course correct, celebrate success, and set new goals accordingly. Remind yourself along the way of the significant reasons why you're doing what you're doing. Everyone wants "more" of something and "less" of something else. You can check in with yourself using the D.R.I.P. system (Discover, Recruit, Individually set expectations around coaching, Persist in coaching).

Make sure that you take notes every time you sit down with yourself or after a session with a coach. It's important to make time for yourself for check-ins every week to make sure that you are staying on track with your goals.

I'm guessing at this point you're realizing that you really are going to need a coach for yourself to keep you on track, keep you accountable, help celebrate your victories, and even to help you figure out what you want and what your goals are in the first place! My door is always open. Even if you don't want me as your coach, find someone.

Remember this—every person you get to manage is also a person you have a chance to lead. Now, it's time for you to get started coaching your team. I know it might seem a little scary, but no one expects you to be perfect at it right out of the gate. The important thing, as with most endeavors, is to start. Experience will come as you go and the longer you delay, the more your employees and your business are suffering. You have it within your power to change a life today. Will you step up and do it? Will you transform from manager to become a true leader who coaches their people? If so, it will change you, and all those who choose to work for you for the best. When the people you develop learn to coach and learn to lead, you are passing your legacy onto others. As such, one day your leadership transformation will change the world.

Appendix

Leadership Acknowledgments

Words can't describe how blessed I am getting to work with the most amazing leaders on the planet. While there's no way I can acknowledge every leader I've ever coached in here, I want to acknowledge those leaders I've spent the most time with over the years around what I respect most about your leadership qualities.

Brittany H. though you're gone, you will forever hold a spot in my heart, and your amazing leadership will never be forgotten.

Shawn H. for all the adversity you've faced, you've had the courage to pick yourself back up, continue to put on a smile, pour into your team while rebuilding your life and your business.

Cynthia C. your willingness to change and grow so that you can be the best leader for everyone on your team and for carrying Brittany's torch into the future.

Ron R. for your desire to ensure Brittany's vision becomes a reality, and your loyalty to the entire Hibdon family.

Sam C. for your perseverance, dedication to excellence, your unwavering faith and love for your team.

Brian M. for your candor, your willingness to grow, and your tenacious skill mastery, and for your fearless approach to selling and leading your team.

Phillip J. for your ability to balance focus and fun, and your competency in the way you run your department, and your willingness to mentor and teach those who want to grow under you.

Tom A. for your dedication to creating a coaching culture throughout your entire organization, for your uncanny skills with data and reporting, and for your coachability and passion for leadership.

Nick P. for trusting and empowering your management team to take your company to new heights, for investing in your people, and for always leading by example.

Hess C. for a senior leader who exemplifies servant leadership, your willingness to make hard decisions for the betterment of the whole, for listening to your team, and for the great care you put into decision making.

Gwen W. for your passion for doing things right, your attention to detail, your mental focus, your desire to be a great coach for your team, and your ability to be in the moment with anyone you're pouring into.

Appendix: Leadership Acknowledgments

Brice G. for your honesty, your willingness to hash out challenging conversations with your team members, and intensity in your efforts.

Brit S. for your confidence to develop people under you to do your role, your tenacity to battle through adversity and still always come to work with a smile.

Mason T. because you prove that you don't need a manager title to be a leader.

Paul S. Jr. for your honesty, loyalty, innovation, creativity, and love for your team that is only matched by your commitment to giving back to your community.

PS3 for your drive, your willingness to listen to your employees, and for your intensity around being the best.

Steven S. for your resilience, your passion, and your ability to hold your people to high standards. Also, the way you always push yourself to achieve more.

Jamil K. for your authenticity, your won't quit attitude, and your relationships with your team.

Melissa J. for your coachability, your fairness, your willingness to take one on the chin and continue driving forward.

Nicole L. for your ability to add value to everyone around you, your consistency, drive, your amazingly thick skin, and care for your team.

Danny F. for your positivity, your enthusiasm, and the team cohesion you bring to the table.

Brian D. for your sense of humor, your uncanny finance skills, your being a team building savant, and your ability to retain employees.

Bill T. you're as cool as the other side of the pillow, direct, and desire to mentor others who work for you.

Joe V. for never giving up, your growth mindset, and your calm cool and collected demeanor.

Bernadette R. for your energy, your care for your team members, and your desire to do great in all you do.

Ron H. for your ability to always prove you can teach an "old dog new tricks", your focus on mastery, and your commitment to personal health and development.

Margie R. for your follow through, attention to detail, your professionalism and support for all the managers on your team.

Appendix: Leadership Acknowledgments

Michael S. for your attention to detail, your coachability, your ability to listen to the team, and your desire to build amazing things.

Andy G. for your loyalty, your willingness to adapt, and for the challenging goals you've set for your department's growth.

Richard R. for your coachability, your drive, and your commitment to step up and lead the team to greater success.

Daniel O. (Just kidding Danielle O.) for your unquenchable thirst for knowledge, your ability to freeze time and get everything done, and for your desire to be an even more amazing leader.

Roy H. for your care and empathy for your team, for the way you analyze issues and address them professionally with your people, and for the amazing culture you're building.

Gilbert Y. for your desire to achieve, your dedication to honing your craft, and your willingness to try new things.

Marcy H. for your desire to leave a better legacy for your family, your vision, and your drive to make partnerships stronger.

Chris H. for your skill mastery, your ability to turn things around, and your positive attitude.

Tony K. for your openness to personal development, your flawless execution of growth plans, and for the time and energy you pour into your team to leave a legacy of success.

Michael M. for you analytic skills, your knowledge of your business, and how you've grown your communication as a leader.

Sheryl O. for your ability to interface with all the departments in your business which is so rare for someone in your role. I know you wouldn't agree with this, but for your amazing patience, and great attitude. I feel blessed that I got to meet Aaron. Remember he is always with you.

Jeff W. my brother, for the love you have for your family, your dedication to your people, your technical competency, your thick skin, your humility and the way you take ownership of failures. The relationships you've established over your lifetime is the ultimate legacy. May your faith continue to grow as the holy spirit fills your heart!

Tanner W. for allowing me to marry you and Maddie! I love you guys so much! For your determination to succeed, for your courage in creating high standards and in challenging the status quo, for your passion for your business, and the dedication to your people. The apple doesn't fall far from the tree in you, sir.

Gale G. though you've been through a lot of pain with your husband, you were always there to train, coach, and hold your people accountable in the best ways.

Kevin N. for the way you trust your people, delegate and empower them to succeed.

Trev O. for your dedication and selfless service to your people, and your loyalty to your company owners.

Steve C. for your strict adherence to process, and your skills at creating business efficiency. Your desire to leave a legacy of success for your company before you retire. Also, for the way you have applied coaching to your life in general.

Donna C. for your willingness to grow as a communicator and leader for your team. It's rare to find leaders humble enough to listen to their people and then dedicated enough to change for them all while consistently putting up top tier results.

Lori N. for your ever positive attitude, how you find new ways to motivate your team, and your strong organizational skills.

Zack J. for your passion for training your team, your willingness to jump in and get involved with clients, and your fun positive attitude.

Phillip C. for the way you've been able to retain your staff and keep them motivated even while battling recalls, recessions, and remodeling.

Nick and Emily F. because you guys are an awesome package deal, for taking work seriously but never letting the stress of management consume you. For the way both of you ramped up your skills to rise to the occasion of leadership.

Red, all the managers in the organization think the world of you, for your family-first mindset, and your empathy for others.

Jay you always say "you can't teach an old dog new tricks", yet every time we talk, you continue to grow as a leader. You've proven that even hardened clay can be shaped into something new.

Don B. for your passion for the business, your extreme competency, your loyalty to your managers, for how much you care for and love your people.

Tom F. for your conviction to success, your ability to adapt, your willingness to try new things, your openness to letting me push you out of your comfort zone, and your growth mindset.

Michelle L. for your steadfast integrity, your conviction to doing things right, your willingness to try management again, and for opening your heart to relational leadership.

Appendix: Leadership Acknowledgments

Tim R. for your high energy, for the ownership you take in the success of each of your employees, and your ability to transform from a telling manager to a leader who asks, listens, and coaches.

Kevin M. for your closeness to your people, your ability to see the good in them, for your willingness to learn, and because of how much you care about the entire company's success.

Bill M. for your dedication to the auto industry, the way you treat your employees like family while also holding firm to your boundaries and expectations. For understanding that your people are assets and the way you invest in them, and your business culture.

Javy C. your positivity, motivation, and love for everyone on your team shines through in all that you do. Your talent as a general manager is only matched by how much you care about your people and your customers. It's been an honor achieving greatness and setting records alongside you for years.

Chris L. for your ability to see the good in everyone, and the way you never give up on one of your employees. I'm grateful for the way that you point me in the right direction and leverage coaching to build your people up. Moreover, your growth mindset is awesome.

Alicia A. for your extreme competency in your role, your growth mindset, your willingness to contribute to others success, and for your passion around being great.

Aaron B. for the way you keep the mood of the team light, and for how much you care about every persons paycheck. Also, for your strength in knowing process, and the dedication to keeping your team

Jason B. for your steadfast loyalty to your company owner, your ability to close Staten Islanders and for your ability to adapt and role with the punches.

Ryan M. for your thirst for knowledge, your ability to maximize profit, and your desire to carry your fathers torch of success into the future.

David S. for your meticulous attention to detail, your professionalism and loyalty to your family and team.

Sophia for the way you support your team, your loyalty to your dealership, and your consistent positive attitude.

Dave F. for your intense focus on building CRM, your willingness to give me a chance to be your team's coach, and for allowing me to work with all your dealerships. It's been very rewarding to be a small part of the growth and success of your company.

Jonathan S. for your unwavering faith, your strong boundaries, your unending thirst for knowledge, your skills as a product manager, and who you are as a person.

Steve R. your energy, enthusiasm, and ability to become "one of us" as it relates to the auto industry. I never doubted you for a moment, and I am so glad we got to work together.

Rachel C. for your care and empowerment for your team. For your dedication to Evolve, your vision for what you know is possible. For the bonds you build with your community. Your business is truly unique, and an echelon above your competition. Never doubt yourself.

Tayler L. for the way you take action, communicate what you need to your business partners, and for your desire to reward loyalty, effort, and ensure your people are paid well and taken care of.

Reid R. for your unquenchable desire to learn, your dedication to personal growth, your commitment to mastering everything you do, for how much you take success personally, for the way you rose to the challenge to support your wife's battle, and for your loyalty to our cause.

Chas K. to see how far you've grown since we've met is amazing. You've grown as a professional, as a coach, and moreover in your confidence. The value you bring to our company is vast, and there isn't enough time in the day for me to recognize you enough for your awesomeness.

Justin D. where do I start! I'm grateful to God that he put us together. You are as "growfective" as they come. In addition to the way that you've transformed as a coach, I respect you for your knowledge, your adaptability, your faith and love for family.

Kelly K. your effort around ensuring our marketing clients are supported is awe inspiring. Your passion for what you do and enthusiasm for the growth of our companies is energizing for all of us. Thank you.

Eric P. you've taken to your role as a coach like a fish to water. Thank you for being so coachable, so caring toward everyone you get to work with, and for taking true "teamership" around our mutual success!

Eddie M. because of your passion for the restaurant business, for how much you give to the community, and the way you've battled adversity and loss to make Maggie O's the best Irish Pub restaurant chain in Missouri.

Doug N. for all the sales management skills you taught me, for your amazing ability to tell a story, and for your willingness to mentor me and teach me the automotive management skills I needed to launch my career.

Appendix: Leadership Acknowledgments

John S. for pouring into me as a young manager and being willing to have those difficult conversations. For always telling me what I needed to hear instead of what I wanted to hear.

Chad C. for your mentorship, for teaching me candor, for supporting my growth as an entrepreneur, and for giving me a shot at running with the big boys in people development. You forever changed my life for the better.

Jim W. for the value you see in questions, your ability to focus and always be efficient, and for allowing my team and I to support your insanely awesome commercial real estate career.

Dean P. for your investment in your people, your ability to consume knowledge, your commitment to your leadership team, and for your support around our projects together.

Skip S. for allowing me into your life, for the culture you created that allowed all those employees to thrive. You and Dean have proven that you can have a successful business and allow people to be with their families.

Jay A. for leading one of the strongest and most talented group of managers to success, for the way you battled to stay on top through acquisitions and turmoil. For your hard charging growth mindset, and the way you never give up.

Flynt J. for your loyalty to your leadership team and people. For your analytical skills, your intuition, and your coachability.

Greg B. the transformation you made was awe inspiring. For the way you went from manager grinder to leader who coached, and how your attitude and passion for your business grew together. Thanks for being awesome.

Kevin A. for your involvement with your team, your unending energy to get stuff done, and for how much fun it is strategic thinking around better processes alongside you.

Bob G. for your ability to listen to your team, care for them, and support your managers around you. You and your family have been through a lot and you never let that affect the way you showed up each day. Much respect.

Brian D. for your faith, and dedication to God. For your conviction for doing things right, and for your growth mindset.

Mike D. for your unmatched desire to be the best, and for the way you challenge every individual on your team to be better.

Josh A. for the way you took the bull by the horns as soon as you were given the management opportunity. You are a gift to the people you lead, and the company you work for. Your conviction to developing your people is only rivaled by the way you take ownership and change to be a better leader for them.

Appendix: Leadership Acknowledgments

Jason S. your ability to be productive and keep everyone around you productive is awesome. I'm grateful for all the opportunity to support you and your career growth. Thank you for being an awesome manager AND leader for your team.

Jay D. your energy, enthusiasm, and ability to always make work fun is only comparable to the long term relationships you establish with your companies customers and your co-workers.

Daniel H. for your mad spreadsheet skills, for your desire to learn everything you can about leadership, and your commitment to personal growth.

Brett D. for your loyalty and the way you've grown as a communicator, manager, and leader throughout our journey together.

Tammy L. your energy is next level, and so is your willingness to be a better communicator and leader. Never doubt the value you bring to your business and your team.

Brandon D. for your humility, your kind heart and your ability to listen. I'm grateful to have been a part of your growth journey.

Travis L. for your innovation, your focus and leadership. Your people believe in you, would take a bullet for you. Thank you for bringing me into the Urban Science and Central Services team. I'm grateful for how well we work together.

Megan L. for your amazingly positive attitude, your confident demeanor, and your ability to listen to your teams needs while empowering them. You rock Megan.

Kelly B. for your ability to cook up motivation for your team (see the Chef pun there?) and how your professionalism makes everyone around you better.

Bill and John S. both of you brothers are a gift to the automotive industry and I am blessed to know you. You guys have hearts of gold, and I commend your ability to remain forever technically competent.

Patrick B. for the way you and the smallest group of managers are able to accomplish so much. For your consistent amazing results you're able to produce, and your understanding of the importance of culture.

Steven M. for your heart of gold, for how well you know your people and for your commitment to treating them great, and investing in them.

Nick for your unwavering commitment to accountability, your passion for leveraging the technology tools at your disposal, and your involvement with your team.

Appendix: Leadership Acknowledgments

Larry P. for your great sense of humor, your intensity to crush it, your coachability and your dedication to achieving growth with your team.

Kim B. for the way you carried the torch for your late husband in your business for years, for how much you care about your people, and for your vision. A convo with you always inspires me.

Bill A. for your confidence, your presence, and your conviction toward pouring into your team members. For all the challenges we overcame together, the way you crushed it right up until the business was sold.

Aimee S. for your positive attitude, your passion for lifting others up, and for the energy, effort and love you put into caring for those you care about.

Steve for your enthusiasm toward your customer experience, for your loyalty to your leadership and your dedication to making every possible deal.

Printed in Great Britain
by Amazon